THE STRUGGLE
WITH GOD

THE STRUGGLE
WITH GOD

by

Paul Evdokimov

Translated by

Sister Gertrude, S.P.

PAULIST PRESS

(Paulist Fathers)

Glen Rock, New Jersey

Contents

III

The Charisms of the Spiritual Life

and

the Mystic Ascension

Introduction

If we know how to listen, we can hear above the noise of the world the questions put to us by the meaning of things. More than ever before, human existence entails the need for clarity and asks the sole question that can be addressed to every man. Beyond all catechetical or propaganda literature, and at the level of a conscience freed from every prejudice, the 20th-century believer is invited to ask: "What is God?" and the atheist, the one who denies, is invited to make clear the object of his negation.

The question causes surprise, and if the answer is slow in coming, the silence is refreshing. This question is revealing for man himself; it is also a way of saying: "Who are you?"

The one who would say God is creator, providence, savior, reviews the chapters of a textbook or gives testimony to a theory, to a dialectic distance between God and himself. God, in this case, is not the All, passionately and spontaneously grasped in the immediate content of his revelation. St. John Climacus, one of the most severe of the ascetics, said we should love God as a young man loves his betrothed.[1] A lover who is passionately in love would say: "But that is all. That is my life. There is nothing but that; the rest does not count; it is non-existent." St. Gregory of Nyssa, at the height of his emotion, let these words escape him: "Thou whom my soul loves . . ."[2]

Atheism rejects only an ideology, a system, a theory, which man has too often misused; it never rejects divine reality, which is revealed only through faith.

Patristic tradition does not attempt any definition of God, for God is beyond all human words. "Concepts create images of God,

[1] *Echelle,* XXX, 3; col. 1156C.
[2] *P.G.,* 44, col. 801A.
[3] *P.G.,* 44, cols. 377B, 1028D.

1

wonder alone grasps something," confessed St. Gregory.[3] For the Fathers, the word *God* is a vocative addressed to the Ineffable.

The difficulty in regard to man is just as great. It caused Theophilus of Antioch to say: "Show me your man and I shall show you my God." [4] The divine mystery is reflected in the mirror of the human mystery. St. Peter speaks of *homo cordis absconditus,* the hidden man of the heart.[5] *Deus absconditus,* mysterious and hidden, has created his vis-à-vis, his other self, *homo absconditus,* mysterious and hidden.

The spiritual life springs forth in "the pastures of the heart",[6] in its free spaces, as soon as these two mysterious beings, God and man, meet there.

"The greatest thing that happens between God and the human soul is to love and to be loved," affirm the great spiritual writers.[7]

"No man sees me and still lives." [8] For the Fathers, this biblical warning meant that we cannot see God with the light of our reason, and that we can never define God, for every definition is a limitation. However, he is closer to us than we are to ourselves. In the depth of his astounding proximity God turns his face to man and says to him: "I am . . . the Holy One." [9] He chooses among his names the one that veils him most. He is even "thrice holy", as the angels proclaim in the *Sanctus,* thus throwing in relief the incomparable and absolutely unique character of divine holiness. Wisdom, power, even love, can find affinities and similarities, but holiness alone has no analogy here below; it cannot be either measured or compared to any reality of this world. Before the burning bush, in the face of the devouring fire of *"Thou alone art holy",*[10] every human being is but "dust and ashes". For this reason, as soon as the holiness of God manifests itself, the hagiophany immediately arouses the *mysterium tremendum,* a sacred fear, an

4   *P.G.,* 6, 1025B.
5   1 Pet. 3, 4.
6   St. Macaire, *Homélies spirituelles.*
7   Kallistos, *P.G.,* 147, col. 860A-B.
8   Ex. 33, 20.
9   Hos. 11, 9.
10   Apoc. 15, 4.

irresistible feeling of the "wholly other".[11] This is not a fear of the unknown, but a characteristic and mystic awe that accompanies every manifestation of the divine. "I will have the fear of me precede you," [12] God says; and again: "Remove the sandals from your feet, for the place where you stand is holy ground." [13]

Having thus marked off the uncrossable abysses that separate the divine from the human, God immediately reveals their mysterious conformity: "Deep calls unto deep," [14] and "As in water face answereth face." [15] God, the lover of man, transcends his own transcendence toward man, whom he draws from his nothingness, and calls him in his turn to transcend his immanence toward the Holy One. Man can do this because divine holiness has willed to take on man's face. Even more, the "Man of Sorrows" shows us the "Man of Desire", the eternal magnet that attracts all love and enters into us in order that we may live again in him. He says to every soul: "Set me as a seal on your heart, as a seal on your arm; for stern as death is love . . . its flames are a blazing fire." [16]

This is why Scripture tells us: "Be holy, for I, the Lord, your God, am holy." [17] When Peter wishes to define the aim of our Christian life, he speaks of our participating in the holiness of God.[18] Likewise Paul, speaking to the Christians, addresses himself to the "saints" of Rome or Corinth. Would he still address himself today to the "saints" of Paris or London? Would the modern believer recognize himself among this group?

As soon as anyone speaks of sanctity, a psychological block is formed. We think of the giants of former days, the hermits buried in caves, stylites perched on columns. These "illuminati", "equal to the angels", no longer appear as belonging to this world. Sanctity seems out-of-date. It belongs to a past that has become strange to us and unadapted to the discontinuous forms, the syncopated

---

[11] See R. Otto, *Le Sacré* (Paris, 1929), p. 22.
[12] Ex. 23, 27.
[13] Ex. 3, 5.
[14] Ps. 42, 8.
[15] Cf. Prov. 27, 19.
[16] Canticle of Canticles 8, 6.
[17] Lev. 19, 2.
[18] 2 Pet. 1, 4; Heb. 12, 10.

rhythms of modern life. Today a stylite would not even arouse curiosity. He would provoke the question: "What good is he?" A saint is no longer anything but a sort of yogi, or perhaps to put it more crudely, a sick or unadjusted person; in any case, a useless being.

Before our eyes the world is losing its sacred character without meeting any resistance. Formerly the sacred was a sign formed by the matter of this world and reflecting a "wholly other", translating this and testifying to its presence by means of the sign. Does this "wholly other" speak to man today? For him the transcendent no longer transcends anything; it has lost all correspondence with the real. It is non-existent. How symptomatic of this brutal fact is the recent appearance of a form of atheism that is *organic* and *normal*. Far from seeming to be a neurosis of civilization, it appears rather to express a certain health, a psychic state free from all metaphysical disquietude, occupied fully with this world, insensible to religion. Such a "profaneness", such a smiling and disillusioned scepticism does not fight against anything. Neither does it any longer ask questions about God. To be intelligent today means to understand everything and to believe in nothing.

At its best, this attitude politely relegates sanctity to the cloister, far from the world of men; this means that the spiritual life scarcely interests modern man. He considers it a useless object hampering him, fit only to be stored in the attic of history.

In addition, there are other attitudes. Even, and perhaps above all, in circles conforming to an established religion, anything religious provokes in sincere souls an immediate reflex of boredom. Boredom with services and ceremonies performed in an archaic language, or with childish hymns proclaiming a joy devoid of meaning, boredom with a symbolism misleading in its hermetic character, the key to which is lost forever.

There is also the world of black-clad clerics, seemingly sinister whether they are traditionalists or progressives, sincere or ridiculous. There is moreover the pious style of rules and restraints with their oppressive gravity. There is the mediocrity of "the good", who take themselves seriously and impose on others their own mentality, formed by edifying discourses and sermons where empty formulas are displayed in a superfluity of words. A religious life that has been domesticated, socialized, democratized, has the least attractive appearance. Its intellectual content is very low, keeping to the level of old-fashioned manuals with their limited ideas and their system of apologetics no longer accepted today. On the world scale it is an enormous social obstacle, reinforcing the dominant ideologies that are hostile or indifferent to anything religious. In the face of revelation, however, it is not a question of man alone, and the miracle of the judgment of faith is produced. In the light of a serious analysis, we quickly discover that, having drawn near each other by their fundamental insufficiency and the metaphysical poverty of their respective visions, the outdated religious man and the modern irreligious man meet back to back in an immanence imprisoned within itself.

I
THE ENCOUNTER

1
Atheism

A theism compels attention and impresses everyone by its massive diffusion. It is no longer the privilege of an enlightened minority, but expresses a norm common to all classes of society. A civilization has been consciously built on a refusal of God, or more precisely, on a negation of all dependence on any power beyond this world. In fact, science no longer has need of God as a hypothesis. Moreover, from the moral point of view, God seems not to be all-powerful since he does not suppress evil, or if he does not wish to do so, then he is not love.

Built thus on a negation, atheism has no metaphysical content proper to itself and no constructive philosophy. Explicitly expressed, it still remains rare. Its dominant and widespread form is an atheism of fact, invertebrate but practical. Philosophic considerations intervene only afterward to justify attitudes or to provide an excuse. Its reasons are never truly rational, and they cannot be, for they fall short. Being of an empirical order, they are utilitarian and pragmatic. This explains why the problem at this level simply ceases to interest man. Since he is more concerned with economic and political questions, religious beliefs no longer mean anything to him. His attitude is strengthened by his often justified distrust of philosophers, who have abdicated and betrayed their social function by their own scepticism.

St. Paul knew well what he was doing when he centered his teaching on what immediately aroused a reaction from the men who relied on discursive reason. Indeed the incarnation is always a folly and a scandal for human thought. The latter in its historic criticism demythologizes and distinguishes between the historic Jesus and the Christ rigged out in the dogmas of faith.

The archaic state of knowledge in past ages makes every scholar mistrustful and little inclined to take into account a so-called

9

"revelation". They find no certitude at the outset of the alleged event and, in every way, a truth buried in the centuries is unacceptable to the contemporary spirit that is interested only in the here and now. One must choose between verifiable facts and texts visibly originating in a myth. To the atheist, it is inconceivable, even offensive, that God should enter into time and confide his truth to a handful of obscure disciples and to the precarious transmission of texts, written twenty centuries ago. The life of Jesus shows only anecdotes and miscellaneous facts without any guarantee of objectivity. Can a contingent fact, scarcely remarked by historians, touch the heart of the man in the street in this 20th century? How can an event dated and fixed in time and space lay claim to an eternal value—the authority of God and the universal importance of the salvation of every man? There is here something monstrously out of proportion,[1] even unbearable for critical reason. The man Jesus could very well have lived in Palestine. It is not so much his divinization by his disciples as the *humanization of God* that is declared impossible. A moral ideal, a philosophic concept could, if need be, receive the title of divine, but the philosopher refuses a God-man, refuses a God speaking as a human being and taking on the face of a man. Thus the authority of the apostolic witnesses crumbles away, and with it, that of the Word. Through lack of hearers, it is more than ever a voice crying in the historic wilderness. Like the wise men of Athens in former times, the man in the street now repulses all discourse with "We will hear thee again on this matter." [2]

We must pay attention to this very real difficulty and we must be clear on what faith requires of us and the why of this requirement. Unfortunately, believers and unbelievers are profoundly ignorant of one another, they do not understand one another, they belong to different anthropological types. Even for St. Gregory of

[1] The man who declared himself God is unsupportable for the Jews and God-become-man is a scandal for the Greeks. The Old Testament knew God but was closed to the idea of a suffering God; the Greek mysteries knew the image of a suffering God, but they did not know God. The New Testament reveals both.
[2] Acts 17, 32.

Nyssa, the man who is not moved by the Holy Spirit constitutes a species, a humanity apart.

Believers naively advance arguments drawn from a fear of judgment or from a metaphysical disquietude in the face of death. On the present level of evolution, the resurrection of the dead and all the traditional problems of the religious man do not even graze the conscience of a certain type of atheist, for in this case of advanced degeneracy, even his subconscious does not bear any trace of them. We are witnessing a profound change in the human substratum.

It is important to understand this for, above the always formless crowd, the existence of a real spiritual life, the fact of a saint, would constitute a kind of thorn in the side for an atheism that wishes to be systematic, moral and totalitarian. Sooner or later the reciprocal ignorance of dynamic faith and militant atheism, as well as their peaceful coexistence, will be shown to be impossible. Messianic apostolates reach a point where they not only exclude one another but violently oppose one another. In fact, there exists already a lucid and serenely authoritarian manner of posing the problem of faith by putting atheism in question in a direct confrontation that permits no cheating, no loophole, no "asylum of ignorance".

Atheism can be explained by the simple fact that God does not impose himself on anyone and that his existence is not immediately evident to all. In the mind of the masses, religious faith is reduced to an exploitation, an alienation, or a compensation. But if we pass beyond this demagogy, a task that is not too hard, we find that criticism comes up against a real difficulty. It is not a question of the indifferent; they do not interest us here. The most surprising thing is the existence, even the possibility, of a conscious atheism. How can one be an atheist?

The word atheism, by its negative *a,* denies theism, denies God. Now the real problem is to show how it can really do this but, first of all, we must specify what it denies. How does atheism define the "complex God" before denying him? This is the whole question. At most it is the negation of a certain type of theology, of an anthropomorphic and human conception of God. This in no way goes beyond the human and in no way does it touch God in himself. On the other hand, to speak philosophically, one can deny a thing only in affirming another. In denying God, what does one affirm in his place? If it is a protoplasm bearing within itself its future prophets, we must confess that this is a hypothesis more problematic than the very simplistic and reasonable idea of a creator God.

To deny, and to be ignorant of, are two very different things. An agnostic affirms nothing and is ignorant of everything. On the other hand, he can deny only proved errors and evident impossibilities. Atheism claims that God is evidently impossible. Now science teaches us to be extremely prudent when we make hypothetical judgments, especially in considering what is impossible. The boundary between the possible and the impossible is changing so constantly that one does not know anymore where to place it. What if the science of tomorrrow should demonstrate that atheism is an impossible deception, an untenable ignorance, a survival of scientistic obscurantism worse than the so-called darkness of the Middle Ages?

Such a complete change of ideas will certainly not take place today. But the glaring absence of an atheistic philosophy that is sufficiently consistent and constructive obliges academic atheism in its recent forms to place itself beyond the problem of God. This is no longer at the end but at its point of departure. That the existence of God is not a philosophic problem is a gratuitous, simplistic and uncritical postulate.[3]

Atheism thus simplified penetrates the masses. It no longer comes from the brains of philosophers and is thus freed from any exercise of the intelligence. Imperceptibly it identifies itself with the historic situation, setting itself up as a consequence of political and economic conditions. It claims and appropriates to itself all efforts against famine, war and injustice. It does this the more easily

---

[3] The term atheism "is more fitting for religious polemics than for philosophic discussions, from where, moreover, it tends to disappear" (de Lalande, *Voc. phil.,* p. 88. For neopositivism, there is no knowledge corresponding to the word God; metaphysical problems are devoid of meaning.

as official religion, having been associated with an order that has passed, now shares its fate, and sees itself thrust aside.

After all, there is no dispute about God in himself. "Let us leave the heavens to priests and sparrows," Heine said. It is his presence in the world, it is his root in humanity that are passionately denied. This negation is made easier by God himself who shows himself but does not prove himself. To speak empirically, it is evident that man can find a fellowman, can even experience an emotion in his regard, without the intervention of the gods. Consequently, at least in appearance, the more a man is a man, the less religious he is and the more he can feel himself the sole demiurge of his destiny and the master of history.

Atheism does not appear anymore as a chance by-product of our human condition; it has become essential, for example, to the *Marxist doctrine*. Communism exists only in function of integral humanism. According to its assumptions, man is the only reality of history. He bears within himself the principle of his own genesis, the creation of man by man. The dialectic relation constitutes history, the relation of the production of man and of the transformation of nature into human nature. Man exists, therefore, only because he has produced himself. From having (the non-plenitude of possessions) he passes to being (ontological plenitude); he appropriates to himself the whole of his being; he creates himself. The "meaning of human" applies only to man, and it arouses the passion of man in regard to man. At the culminating point of his consciousness, liberty is revealed and imposes itself in the "understood necessity" of the creation of its own substance, the production of the total and universal social man.

What is important to understand is that militant atheism is pre-Communistic; it is clearly marked out by its own limits. The denial of God, the proofs for his non-existence, the philosophic exposé of the contradictions inherent in religion, constitute the preliminary dialectic, the *praxis* or action. Facing this, there is inevitably a sphere of abstraction. Man in the period of militant atheism, even the one who expresses it the best, is still an abstract man, for criticism, though Marxist, is a purely intellectual operation.

At the moment when all forms of alienation will be radically suppressed, religious alienation will automatically be suppressed, without the need of any supplementary act. Absolute humanism is effectively atheist; here is the situation in fact.

At the end of historic evolution there will be no place for a militant atheism, for once its objective—the *telos*—is attained, the religious question of the existence of God will not even arise and, at the same time, the period of abstract and theoretic atheism will have been definitely completed. Religion, theism and atheism will share the same lot; they will become museum pieces. Indeed, in the golden age the act of individual conception would be a total generic act. It would be self-sufficient and in it the whole law of the species would be concentrated and totally present to such a degree that the question of the first ancestor would be meaningless. Every question on the subject of origins turns aside from experience, takes a step backward toward a former reflective stage. It puts man and matter again in question and, in so doing, renders them fully non-existing; it is the avowal of their non-essential character. Communism is not a philosophic postulate but an act that completes history. The coming of socialistic man is its unique proof; being irrefutable, it will be more than a proof, it will be a revelation. This is why Communism begins *after* atheism; it is the *praxis,* the transformation of the world. The practical denial of God completed *in actu* is situated once for all at the beginning of the new era.

The denial of God has permitted the affirmation of man. Once this affirmation is made actual, there is no longer anything to be denied or subordinated. The psychological state of Communistic man suppresses the speculative atheism of negation, and the circle is closed on man, on his substance that has been made absolute and divine. On this level total man will not be able to ask a question on his own reality, just as God does not put a question to himself.

As one perceives immediately, the method is simplistic and prephilosophic. The invisible transcendent is decreed to be non-existing, not directly, but in function of matter, because it would diminish the reality and integrity of material fact; it would escape the essential objectivity of consciousness. Furthermore, and this is very serious, once established, integral Communism in suppressing critical atheism would suppress the very conditions that permitted its access. Therefore, it would suppress all possible verification of its own foundation. Critical atheism is only a postulate of a truth which suppresses it without any possible return. The final act annihilates the conditions of its own actualization.

Before the arrival of the total man, denial of God is not sufficient; it is only pragmatic. After his arrival, it is non-existent. Therefore, at no moment is it valid in itself. Right and fact are on two different planes, and the division between them makes it impossible to appeal from one to the other. This flagrant lack of a dialectical bond renders the atheistic demonstration of the Marxists extremely weak, incoherent and untenable in the face of a serious philosophical investigation.

Effective atheism is thus more than atheism; it is an entirely different thing, for it rests on something beyond atheism and its problems. It is accessible only to future man. Therefore, it does not yet exist, and it will not until there is a fully developed Communism. *A fortiori* it is not accessible to a non-Communist. It is clearly the fetishism of matter that makes the god-man come forth from its depths.

This vision explains the present situation in Russia where a certain place is left to the Church as well as to the virulent criticism of religion. These are facts inherent in the pre-Communist stage. We witness a desperate struggle from which critical atheism can extricate itself only by projecting the incredible fabrication of a future myth.

The stronger Marxism is politically and economically, the weaker it is philosophically. The matter of Marxism has nothing in common with the matter of modern physics. When Marx said, with a certain lyricism, that the spirit is "the torment of matter", he dates and manifests an outmoded romanticism. A sharply defined intellectual regression forces Marxism to be only a very archaic form of pancosmic monism. Indeed it presents an emanative philosophy of the totality of matter. The social collective is the only concrete thing of organized existence. Whatever deviates from this "general line" that marks the contours of the socialist pleroma—an individual, for example, or a person wishing to detach himself from it, or worse still, to oppose it—immediately becomes a heretical abstraction. God, not being able to become one of its elements, hinders totalization, and thus reveals himself as the abstraction *par excellence*.

The Marxist totality expels the being of God, but lays claim to the possession of all divine attributes. We recognize here very paradoxically the ontological argument of the Marxists: at the extreme, perfection and existence coincide in the state of divinized protoplasm.

This totalitarian character of Marxism makes it a substitute religion. Marx created the myth of the collective proletariat-messiah, the only class free from the original sin of exploitation; by its sufferings this chosen people expiates, saves humanity and leads it toward the promised land of the kingdom.

Matter attains its peak in the infallible consciousness of Karl Marx. His doctrine is immutable and universal truth. It applies to this earth but also to the innumerable worlds in the universe, matter being everywhere identical. Marxist metamorphosis asks a question that has no possible answer: How did matter evolve toward consciousness, how did it become capable of feeling itself and knowing itself as super-matter? What kind of head had that astonishing first ape who discovered himself to be man, and what was the state of his soul? [4] Here "the more comes forth from the less", and the effect contains that something, that "indefinable something" of which there is no trace in the premises. This is characteristic of a miracle. Matter endowed with self-movement, the cause of which no one can determine, directs itself relentlessly not toward the absurd but toward the *logos* of super-matter.

In its impulse toward self-criticism, Communism today confesses that it has neglected man alone and his solitude. This is the favorite subject of present-day Soviet novels. Whitehead, a great mathematician, said precisely that "God is what man makes from his solitude . . ." Slowly but surely, the surprising idea strikes this

---

[4] One may suppose that those who affirm that man is descended from an ape really do come from one, and those who claim they are children of the heavenly Father are the children of God. One can suppose also that at the lowest point to which he fell, man had engendered the ape.

man: to be opposed to someone is to render homage to his existence.

In the light of a serious analysis, dialectic materialism appears anti-dialectic, retrograde and anti-modern, for it solves the problem of God without having propounded it correctly. It solves it against man, against a fundamental fact of his being. It is a frustration and an alienation in reverse. God is deprived of the human, he is disincarnated. One wonders what man has gained in exchange and what is going to happen when, reversing the view of Feuerbach, God will become conscious of his impoverishment and will definitely appropriate to himself the human—the *totus Christus*—and that will be the judgment.

"Give man this world and the need of another will disappear," is the expression of the demagogic pretension of the atheist to dispose of this world. The *praxis*, substituted for truth, emphasizes efficiency and production in technical areas; it explains its momentary successes, which are always possible but always provisory, being suspended in the "pauses" of history and in the balance sheet of its failures.

In Soviet Russia, the Church declares that it accepts science and its techniques in their totality, the existence of God and the atheist mystique not being scientific questions. It admits in principle the full agreement of religion and science and accepts without any objection the community of goods, preoccupation with one's neighbor, and peace on earth—all these being evangelical truths. Such an attitude disarms and disorganizes critical atheism, which no longer has valid arguments. The bishops refer calmly to history and say: "In spite of the faults and errors of Christians, Christianity still exists; it will always exist, for eternity works for us, for every man, and for time."

Scientism represents a rather widespread form of methodological atheism. However, its simplistic vision risks making the soul sterile, incapable of any religious fruitfulness. This danger comes from the cultural and technical context of present-day life. In the long run it exercises a pressure and a hold on persons who are unaware of it; they breathe it in, as it were, in all public places.

The sectarian and semi-scientific mentality of scientism is displayed on all the pages of the popular press. Closed to all ideas that go beyond it and to all transcendence, scientism, by its methods, makes an effort to account for the world without the intervention of the gods. The universe is formed by the groping extension of life. Man is in a state "of becoming"; starting from the initial facts, everything can be explained, and every existent being is only a partial accomplishment of the possibilities inherent in things. In penetrating the secrets of nature, man does not in any way prove that God does not exist; he simply ceases to feel the need of doing so.

In spite of its apparent optimism, scientism today has burnt its wings in reaching its own limits too quickly. It is no longer dogmatic nor does it promise happiness to man. It has shown that it is powerless to resolve conflicts, to console suffering, or to say: "Rise up and walk." It has lost its power of attraction. In the place of truth, it offers only solutions that are momentarily practical, or it hypnotizes the crowd for a few seconds by the distracting range of its techniques. Like a sorcerer's apprentice, it is outstripped by the famous "possibility inherent in things". It is by no means master of the future, and it knows anguish in the face of the unknown. A person of this type, being warped and narrow in his views, has difficulty in understanding why a surgeon in operating discovers no trace of the soul, or why an astronaut does not see angels passing by him in the sky. That souls and angels are spiritual realities, invisible by their very nature, does not even cross his mind. Can a being living in three dimensions deny the existence of a sphere which goes beyond these three, and which would be precisely one that shows the "possibility inherent in things"? The adventurous minds of mathematicians are fortunately not hampered by such limitations.

The causalist vision considers the interior of a being as a copy of its exterior and thus misunderstands the irreducible novelty of the spiritual activity. Even Marxist dialectics goes beyond simplistic causalism for it shows the interdependence of human consciousness and history. One acts on the other, and their reactions are never passive. Depth psychoanalysis adds to this vision by showing that the biopsychological is not solely a product of the factors at work but a reaction and a *creative expression* of man. Besides an external causality, there exists an internal dynamism, a finality sought for by the intelligence, a conscious and reasonable intentionality. To all that is "by", there is added a "for"; to every affirmation "This is not that", is added "This is that, and more than that". A statue, for example, is only marble, but it is also beauty and harmony. A human being is only a biochemical process, but he is also a mind and a child of God. On a cause there is always grafted a motivation. The causal vision explains man as the product of bio-psycho-sociological structures, but the same elements are ambivalent. They explain but also *express* man, speak of his aspirations and of his projects which go beyond him and transcend the scientistic vision.

Science today no longer assimilates the higher to the lower. It recognizes the thresholds of different levels and planes. When phenomenology inclines toward the affirmation of the continuity of planes, implied one in the other and reducible one to the other, when it affirms "that is that and nothing but that", it goes beyond the descriptive method and passes on to an ontology of pure contingency and of closed world. Now the radical distinction of orders, in Pascal's meaning of the word, remains unmistakably evident. It is not in the concept of matter that materialism can find sufficient reason for a denial of God and of the transcendent. The converse is also true; it is not on matter that a believer bases his faith in God. No scientific method, not even that of materialism, is opposed to the superior that is different in nature and radically irreducible. It thus leaves the metaphysical plane entirely open.

True science affirms soberly and honestly that it offers only an hypothesis giving a satisfactory interpretation of the known facts, an interpretation that is provisory and in constant revision. The scientific rationalism of immanence alone is never sufficient or decisive. In an atheistic scientist, the current objections against religious faith are mingled with affective motivations. The so-called objectivity of a scientist is a myth. He always has his human reactions and, at most, his attitude can be reduced to agnosticism.

Science does not at all stress the reason of the heart or a meta-physical choice.

For a scientist like Einstein, the study of life suggests the ir-resistible idea of order. "I have met nothing in my science that I could oppose to religion," he said. True science is humble; it knows that each of its explanations only places the difficulty elsewhere. "The greatest mystery is in the very possibility of a little science." [5] All of science is a great mystery. "The greatest emotion that we can experience is mystic emotion. This is the seed of all true sci-ence." [6] Lavelle [7] speaks of "the total presence" that awakens the attitude of prayer, and with René Le Senne,[8] philosophic meditation is transmuted into prayer.

The so-called *ex officio* atheism of scientists is definitely out-moded. The more scientific a man is, the more repugnant he finds the absurd and the more he postulates a meaning to the world, even if he cannot formulate it scientifically. He leaves this task to other competencies while keeping a profound respect in face of the mystery. To quote Einstein once again: "The most in-comprehensible thing in the world is that the world is compre-hensible." What the intelligence grasps can never be God; at most it is only the imprint of his glory, the luminous traces of his wisdom. The intelligence can embrace the concomitant intelligibles of the mystery; it can never elucidate the mystery itself. When the re-sources of the intelligence are exhausted, when its last arrow—myth—is sent to the very heart of being, the mystery, without al-lowing its nature to be penetrated, can become enlightening.[9] It can arouse the presentiment of something of immense importance. The mystery is not what we understand, but what understands us.

Existentialist philosophy appears more nostalgic than aggressive. Its pessimism seems to be deliberate. An aphorism of Heidegger expresses a certain virility in despair: "Man is a powerless god."

5 P. Franck, *Einstein, sa vie et son temps.*
6 L. de Broglie, *Continu et discontinu,* p. 98.
7 *Présence Totale.*
8 *Obstacle et Valeurs; Le Devoir.*
9 Gabriel Marcel.

Unquestionably all goes back to Kierkegaard and to his violent reaction against Hegelian rationalism. Hegel's panlogic speculation introduces no harmony into the real, and it offers no salvation. Kierkegaard centered his very personal and very concrete reflection on the religious question: What must I make of myself; in other words, what must I do to be saved?

He built up a most penetrating vision of self-knowledge and anticipated depth psychology. In the depths of the soul he discovered anguish and a feeling of *a priori* guilt which divide a human being and instill an infernal element into him. It is at this level that a thirst for salvation springs up. The ultimate alternative sets the choice between nothingness and the absolute. It offers the greatness of faith contemplating Christ, who has made himself the contemporary of every soul. On the other hand, to flee idealistic metaphysics is to flee the judgment of God.

Reason can function only between the beginning and the end, therefore it is placed between the two. This is why the intermediary sphere of the immanent has no ontological foundation. Only anguish in the face of nothingness can shatter the immanent and lead toward the religious "wholly other". It is because he is "other" that he requires the crucifixion of reason and appeals to "the crucified judgment". The case of Abraham illustrates how morality is transcended by the folly of the cross. Since then the only true witness to the truth is the martyr. Man in himself is only a passover. Now the pascal resurrection-passage of the *transitus* brings about the transcendence whereby death is made Christian; it is no longer an intruder, but the great initiator into the great mystery of eternity.

However, dialectic theology, the theology of the cross, is not yet a theology of the Parousia. The God of Kierkegaard, like the God of Jaspers, remains an absolutely transcendent God. Man is not in God and God is not in man; man stands *before* God. His tragic thirst is not assuaged; he does not yet know all the mystery of the immanent God and the mystic espousal of every soul with God. Kierkegaard did not know that in marrying Regina Olsen his soul could have espoused Christ.

Heidegger took up the formula: man is the existent ego. Existence precedes essence, which means that man creates himself, that no essence determines his destiny; consquently he has no nature but he has a history.

Thrown into co-being with others, finding himself always "in situation", the average man does not oppose the world. Now his cares, an immediate element of life, disperse his attention, direct it toward "non-being", and veil the real. Alienated from himself, he loses his true ego and veers toward the impersonal and anonymous —expressed by "one", *das Man.* Constructed by man's cares, the world is illusory, deceitful, ghost-like, for cares make us forget the real, namely, the ego and its liberty. That is why the ego does not emerge except on the background of nothingness, on that crude screen where the inevitable experience of death is projected. This is the tragedy of man.

It is because by themselves nothingness and freedom are without reason and without foundation; they are limitless and therefore correlative and related. In fact, liberty is limited only by nothingness; it experiences its bounds only in the feeling of death which is essentially concrete, personal and inevitable. Only by transcending his cares toward death is man offered the experience of absolute freedom.[10] Even more, and this is essential, awareness of death arouses and imposes the decision to realize all the possibilities of liberty and thus to assume the full responsibility of the ego faced with its own destiny.

Man in the metaphysical emotion caused by anguish in the face of death experiences the finiteness of his temporal being, but he grasps above all his "non-being", evident as soon as it was founded on his cares and preoccupations. We understand then the fundamental thesis of Heidegger, which can be reduced to the celebrated formula, *Freiheit zum Tode,* freedom toward death; man's tragic grandeur reveals to him his *Sein zum Tode,* his being toward death.

Man's ethical task consists in transcending the world of his cares toward the heroism of that freedom which is responsible for his destiny. This moral teaching is closely related to the ethics of

[10] See the dialectic of Kirilov in *The Possessed* by Dostoievski.

the Stoics. Powerless mortal man is declared to be a god. Not responsible for the being imposed upon him, he assumes his liberty of evaluation and thereby assumes his destiny, whatever may be the final results. He imposes on himself the duty of judging. His freedom is not then purely arbitrary, but he remains a powerless judge through want of an objective criterion of judgment, that is, an axiology of values in function of the Absolute. Is this not the penitent judge of Camus' *The Fall*?

Only an extreme and profound subjectivism, one that is serious and truly tragic, can condition such a vision. The philosophy of nothingness is a theology without God, the place of God being granted to nothingness, and the characteristic of nothingness is to annihilate, or *to nothingize*. Such an impasse, however, could become salutary. Heidegger will never write the second volume of *Sein und Zeit* (*Being and Time*), for he has remarked that his philosophy is not an explanation but a description, and that it is not a denial of God but a certain expectation.[11]

Sartre continues Heidegger's theses. His psychoanalysis constructs a mythology of the *en-soi* and the *pour-soi,* of being and nothingness. The vision is complicated because being is divided and nothingness is multiple. On the plane of being, the *en-soi* is irreconcilable with the *pour-soi*; they establish and destroy each other reciprocally. The union of these two realities, or the convergence of essence and existence, is declared impossible; this is a radical denial of the idea of God, who is this very union.

The *pour-soi* (conscience, idealism), dynamic and changing through its choices, appears as a fissure in the static *en-soi* (being, realism). To establish oneself means to deny the static order, to deny above all, one's own immutability. In affirming its freedom as independence of the world and of the *en-soi,* the *pour-soi* effects negation, annihilates ceaselessly and thus enlarges the gap of non-being in the static being of the *en-soi* and places it at the limit of nothingness.

The denial of a beginning and of an end, both transcendent,

[11] See *Holzwege, Ist Gott tot?*

renders freedom tragic, places it outside pardon, which is possible at the beginning, and outside justification, which is possible at the end. Between the massive existence of a world deprived of meaning, where every value is artificial and irremediable, and the human mind inhabited by the exigency of its reason, the rift is inevitable. There remains to man only the freedom to deny a world that denies him.

Man is terribly alone in his fearful and absolute freedom for which, as in Heidegger's philosophy, he experiences full responsibility. In thus making freedom the formal element of truth (when it is a condition of it) he arrives logically at the affirmation: "Man is condemned to liberty." Condemned because he is not the creator of his being, and free because he is wholly responsible. Sartre clearly belongs to the great French school of moralists.

The analysis of bad faith shows the failure of communication. This is because each *pour-soi* tends to transform another *pour-soi* into an *en-soi,* to make of a subject an object. In the end, he risks transforming himself into an *en-soi,* to petrify himself in a static state by his memories and projects. We either take possession of another or we are possessed by him. Our relationship to another is always deceitful, and that is why other people are hell for us.

If Marxism is a philosophy of totality, Sartrian existentialism is just the opposite; it is the philosophy of what cannot be made total. According to it, totality expresses the ultimate abstraction; on the contrary, the concrete is the individual. Its reality is in function of the gap, the discontinuous, the absurd and the free will. We can understand how the whole idea of God, of the one who fills in the gaps, makes unity out of plurality, and gives meaning to things, would diminish the tragedy of existence, suppress solitude, limit the arbitrary and lessen the sense of autonomous responsibility.

We must give heed to this existential speculation, which, from a philosophic point of view, is very powerful. It overthrows the smug optimism of religious philosophies according to which evil serves the good and in so doing is non-existing as evil; this would render the death of God on the cross incomprehensible. For Sartre, God would diminish the radicalism of evil, of misfortune, of guilt. We can recognize here Kantianism become a religion, but having lost the postulate of the practical reason; it is a Kantianism without God. Kantian rigorism would here attain its climax. The idea of God would contradict the absolute of moral exigency, and it is this absolute character that requires a morality without the Absolute. The greatest paradox is that despair at its height necessarily refers to the Absolute that has been declared impossible. Tacitly, in order to retain its grandeur, existence is a cooperator of value, and thus the ontological argument is denied and described simultaneously. In the last analysis, it is the absence of God that makes the world absurd and hopeless. Therefore, this absence alone justifies the extreme positions of existentialism. Certainly there is no answer to the question posed by this relationship; there is not even a question, for there is no "judge" in this world without finality. Nevertheless, God serves here as a point of reference, although negatively; all is thought of in relation to the absence of the divine meaning. Dostoievski has shown that suffering in its extremes can pass into a complacency in suffering, and that from this state no return is possible; the pleasure of suffering suppresses every solution capable of transcending it.

The more free a man is the more alone he is and the more a stranger to the world. In the rarefied air of the heights, the permanent act of establishing himself, of inventing himself, dominates man's fear and despair. Does it give him the right to be the supreme arbiter? If God does not exist, is everything permitted? For Sartre, who understands this formidable question of Dostoievski, the sufficient reason for ruling out crime resides in the absolute of liberty, which is related to values, even if the latter are contingent and contrived. Because being is to be-with, it has a side that touches the existence of others. When a man posits himself, he at the same time posits others. To be free and to remain upright and sincere, is to posit oneself morally; it is to be in good faith. A criminal, on the contrary, destroys the integrity of his being and of his choice; he is in bad faith.

The being in situation is inserted into history, and since Marxism offers a meaning of history in its theory of social evolution, Sartre seeks in it possible human communication. The abyss of liberty, very strangely, arouses dizziness, disgust, nausea. One would say that the deception pays off. This is what Dostoievski has indeed foreseen, saying that man will never be able to bear the yoke of freedom and that Marxism offers the maximum possibility of getting rid of this royal gift. Sartre confesses: "I lead to nothing, my thought does not allow me to construct anything; then there is no other solution but Marxism" (*La critique de la raison dialectique*). The difficulty, however, remains without a solution. Marxism exaggerates the importance of matter in order to make it creative. Existentialism, on the other hand, makes it blind in order better to fight against it and to hold man in check.

Nietzsche, and Sartre in his wake, have proclaimed the death of the adversary without ever succeeding in definitely eliminating him. His shadow pursues them; the reverse of God is indeed present in man's every thought. Man's drive toward the superman is thwarted by his impotence and is defeated. Freud had discovered the mysterious original fault, the "death of the Father". The man who brought it about could never overcome his remorse, and this is the origin of the collective neurosis. The profound pessimism of the last works of Freud comes from his tardy clairvoyance. His utopia of human happiness had crumbled away, and his resignation was bitter. Moreover, the superman came to nothing, and the closed humanism of the atheists is doomed to failure.

Malraux in his *Métamorphose des dieux* declares that in order to invent and to start his own divinization, man has to conquer his obsessive complex of the Absolute. Can he do this? Freud as a psychotherapist answers negatively. According to Sartre, man kills God in order to say: "I am, therefore God does not exist." But even for Sartre, this power of liberty manifests its emptiness and the vanity of nothingness. Gide wished his moral teaching to be more consistent. His only principle was that a man should go to the limit of himself, to conform *sincerely* to the standards which each one would give to himself according to his free choice.

However, the impunity that every atheist enjoys during his earthly existence is not the last word; death jealously hides its mystery. The devil told Ivan Karamazov the story of an atheist who after death perceived that reality was different from his advanced ideas. "I do not accept it, it contradicts my convictions," he cried, and lay down across the road. He was condemned to walk until his chronometer would decompose into its elements.

In answering Sartre, Merleau-Ponty [12] said that man is not condemned to freedom; he is condemned to meaning, in other words, he is called upon to decipher the meaning of existence and, above all, the meaning of freedom itself.

We must recognize the grandeur of existentialism that has centered all its reflection on freedom. Fundamental evidence of the human mind, freedom constitutes the creative activity of man. Now in this function, unless it contradicts itself, it cannot come from the world with its system of dependencies and constraints. It is evident that freedom is transcendent to the world, has its origin elsewhere, and is offered as a *royal gift*. That is why in his profound philosophy Jaspers designates clearly the *Giver* and bears powerful witness to the existence of God. Jaspers' great merit is his discovery of a proof of divine existence in freedom. We find there the fatherland of freedom, where it has its roots, and in this way it effects an opening toward God. God inspires it to be truly free; this renders it different in every respect from the type of dependence found in Kantian theonomy. God has created a *"second freedom"*. To this gift of God man answers by the gift of himself; he dies and rises in the convergence of these two freedoms, and by this experience he has access to the meaning of his existence. His freedom is never an object for man. It is not even action, but rather a creative reaction to the Giver, to his invitation to become a freedom of service and to testify to its heavenly origins.

There still remains a rather widespread form of atheism: *psychologism*. This attitude of mind tends to see in every religious sentiment a function of the soul, a subjective psychological datum. It thus reduces religion to a causality productive of aims or to the sublimation of an instinct. Every expression of man brings us back to our present reality, but it also expands it and leads to what will make us more fully ourselves. It breaks the vicious circle

[12] *Phénoménologie de la perception,* p. XIV. According to the Gospel, it is the truth, the *meaning* that makes man free.

of immanence and refers to the transcendent. Here the role of depth psychology and the genius of Jung are decisive. Jung has demonstrated that the religious symbol testifies to a reality that is at the same time intra-human and trans-human. Even in clinical cases, the symbol always bears traces of trans-subjective archetypes. The judgment of truth refers not only to the causal order but to the order of meaning. Disorders come from the meanings that have been imposed on a man but that he has not assumed for himself. Normally, a man ought to discover freely *what he is* and to give himself his own proper meaning. This is why, according to Jung, the fundamental problem for all the sick is the *religious attitude*. "All have become sick from the fact that they had lost what living religions have always given to their faithful." [13] Jung declares as a certainty that every life has a meaning, and the task of the doctor is to lead his patient to this discovery. This entails a clear religious awareness. "The one who has passed through this can calmly say: 'It was a grace of God'." [14] "The man who has experienced it possesses an inestimable treasure and a source that provides a meaning to life."

It may be that modern atheism is providential in showing us the urgent need there is to *purify* our idea of God, and to raise the dialogue to a biblical and patristic plane, above all systems of the theology taught in the schools. Here Jung's message takes on breadth and importance. The future depends on the trans-subjective spiritual content of the human psyche: *With what and by what* will man live his destiny? The quaternity of which Jung speaks is an application of the dogma of Chalcedon ("without confusion and without separation") to the mystery of the eighth day, to the apocatastasis or final restoration of all beings to God. The consubstantiality of all creatures is opposed to fragmentation. The saints and martyrs before the throne of the Lamb await the final change from dissimilarity to resemblance. Origen [15] insists on this, saying that Christ is waiting for his glory to shine forth in the totality of his body. If this still remains a mystery, it is clear, however, that

[13] *Die Beziehungen der Psychotherapie zur Seelsorge*, p. 16.
[14] *Psychologie und Religion*, p. 188.
[15] *In Levit., hom.* 7, n. 2.

only love can break the heart of matter from within; but to do this, it must, following the example of Christ, descend to it.

Jung tells us this as a psychologist.[16] It is his last word, his final testament. Here he goes beyond science, suppresses psychologism, and attains the grandeur of a prophet of the last days. By his words, Job gives us the answer that he finally received. It is for Job's friends, believers and atheists, to give heed.

By the absence of a positive content, all forms of atheism lead to a systematic deception. The existence of evil hinders atheism from becoming a solution. The irrational character of suffering and of death keeps reason in check and shows its failure. Indifferent to good and to evil, nature is so also to man and to his destiny; she crushes him by her absurdity. The sole efficacious solution would be to postulate ignorance of freedom. Only on this condition would evil and suffering be suppressed since one would suppress consciousness of them. A puppet has no right to tragic tears, but every form of resignation is felt to be nothing but an unendurable abdication of man.

Father Valensin [17] carries his reflection to its limit. If, by an impossibility, evidence would be given that there is no God, "I would think I would be honoring myself in believing it, for if the universe is something idiotic and despicable, it is so much the worse for him; the wrong was not in me for having believed that God is, but in him for not existing." At this high level, the absence of God for man is infinitely more important than the presence of the world; that is, that this absence is unthinkable. This is not because of a simple longing, nor a solution of anguish, nor Pascal's wager, it is evidence for every *adequate reflection*. The problem of evil was a stumbling block to Jewish theology: Christ did not suppress evil, therefore he is not the true Messiah. This is also the argument of atheism: Christ has not brought to pass the kingdom of God on earth. The Gospel has never promised any material happiness on earth. It is profoundly pessimistic in regard to history, for if freedom is real, it is so also for evil. The deliverance of which the

16 *Die Antwort auf Hiob.*
17 *Autour de ma foi* (1948), p. 56.

Gospel speaks is never the mechanical destruction of evil, but a *cure,* and Christ "has conquered death by death". As long as the last human being has not freely participated in this victory, evil will continue to condition history. God could take our place in order to suffer and to die, but he cannot do so *for our acts* of freedom, of choice and of love. Liberty frees only the one who desires it. That is why the one who desires nothingness will have it in his own way, at least for a fleeting moment. No human exigency equals the divine exigency for freedom for man. This is what forms God's hell before forming man's hell, and that is why God descends there.

The Christian position is decisive here. Apologetic pragmatism does not treat the problem of evil in itself, but as a necessary component of the world. Evil has an astonishing power; it has drawn God forth from his silence and has made him pass through death and resurrection. It is still the existence of evil that is the most striking proof of God's existence. A world that puts to death the just and innocent Socrates [18] calls for another world, and bears testimony to a beyond where Socrates reappears and the risen Christ will inaugurate eternity. "Atheism shows force of mind, but only up to a certain degree," Pascal noted.[19] No denial of God reaches God, for it is situated outside him; it is a negation of a false god or of an abstract conception of God. No one can invent God, for no one can go toward God unless he starts from him. Ontological truth precedes noetic truth and is presented under the form of experimental evidence.

The error of every criticism of the ontological argument for the existence of God is to see in it a deduction of being from the content of thought. St. Anselm never meant this. It is a question of intuition seizing the impossibility of thinking certain contents as pure contents of consciousness.

The idea of the absolute is *inalienable.* Every philosophical thought has the absolute in view and reflects in relation to the absolute. God thinks God. If a man thinks God, he is already within

[18] Justin sees in the trial of Socrates a prefiguration of the trial of Jesus.
[19] *Pensées,* n. 225, p. 431, in British edition.

the divine thought on God, he is in the evidence that God has of himself.[20] The content of the thought on God is not a content that is only thought. In every thought of God, it is God who thinks himself in the human mind and who constitutes immediately the experience of his presence. Man cannot yet say anything of God, but he can invoke him and cast himself into his presence.

Between the impossibility of denying and the impossibility of proving is situated this irrefutable experience with its unshakable evidence. If every thought is always in relation to God and has him in view, every thought on existence that becomes an argument affirms the existence of God. As Péguy said: "One must do violence to oneself not to believe." [21] An interiorized conception of the ontological argument [22] could indeed trace the way to God of every modern man.

It may be that the world is now more than ever near religious faith. Science no longer presents any difficulty, and atheism can advance no serious argument. However, there is a considerable obstacle that comes from Christianity itself. It is the *latent atheism of believers*.

On the threshold of faith, the enduring freshness of words such as: "I have set before you life and death, the blessing and the curse",[23] invites us to most serious reflection. It is a question of choosing our destiny. At the opposite pole of *no,* which engenders numberless heterogeneous groups and separations, there is the unconditional *yes* which turns all into an infinity of unions. St. Paul says: "Only 'yes' was in him." [24] In this *yes* the fiat of man answers the fiat of the creator, and since Pentecost, it is directed toward the last day. On the dial of history, the hour of messianic restoration may sound at the most unexpected moment as the Gospel tells us. To hear it, and more especially to be able to listen to the interior march of history, we must attain that depth of silence

[20] "In the saint it is God who speaks from his depths" (*Philocalie*).
[21] *Porche du Mystère de la deuxième vertu,* Oeuvres complètes, p. 175.
[22] See our study, "L'aspect apophatique de l'argument de saint Anselme," in *Spicilegium Beccense* (1959).
[23] Deut. 30, 19.
[24] 2 Cor. 1, 19.

below which, according to Kierkegaard, "man has neither eyes nor ears". For this reason the Gospel ceaselessly returns to the warning: "He who has ears let him hear."

Simone Weil noted that there are two kinds of atheism, one of which is a purification of the idea of God. In a certain sense this is a grace. The Church is invited to present to men a "showing" of the true God. It can begin an "ecumenical" dialogue with the atheist, because atheism is clearly a Christian heresy. It has never approached faith in its essence, and has never contested it in its mysterious reality as gift of God; believers and historic expressions of faith are in question.

If empirical conditions favor unbelief, it is because in our day man will no longer tolerate any abdication of his rights nor any mandate over him. There is here a very positive element that we must take seriously, namely, the refusal of any recognition of God that would not be at the same time recognition of man. Atheism obliges Christians to correct the flagrant faults of the past and to recognize man and God at the same time, to show in God a *human epiphany.* Abraham's faith made him confess that with God all things are possible. The Christian's faith implies that with man also all things are possible.

For the apostles and saints, relation with God was always concomitant with that of man. In the modern dialogue between atheists and Christians, Marxist atheism of solidarity must be answered by the man of the ecclesial community, and atheistic existentialism of solitude must be answered by the monk.

It is necessary to disengage the Gospel message from all historic and social context that is out-of-date. Our age, as Simone Weil has said, is in need of "a sanctity that has genius".

It would be a grave error to assign only negative characteristics to our age. Man grows in the measure of his exigencies. Religious ideas are deepened in the same proportion. History moves toward a final interrogation on God and man, and these two form only one mystery of divine love. The tensions can end in an apocalyptic outburst. At the worst, it will be the *maranatha,* and the stones will cry out the terrible prayer of the agonizing like an accompaniment to the last martyrs.

2
Faith

F aith bears within itself an obstacle which, inherent in its very
enigmatic nature, is in exact proportion to its grandeur: "God
is in heaven and you are on earth." [25] This distance, unbearable in
the long run, formerly made Isaiah utter the profoundly human
cry: "Oh, that you would rend the heavens and come down." [26]
The often forced optimism of our hymns does not resolve the
secret feeling of an absence that one fears to avow.

How can we pass from an abstract, distant and catechetical
knowledge to a personal encounter, to a living communion? How
can the presence of God enter the lives of man? "Why does God
make faith so difficult?" asks the man who is the prey of doubts.
The resurrection had inaugurated "the eighth day", yet in appearance nothing has changed. The new world has been inserted in
the old, and the eighth day exists only in the seven others. St. Peter
knew the skeptical and mocking spirit that asked: "Where is the
promise of his coming? For since the fathers fell asleep, all things
continue as they were from the beginning of creation." [27] Likewise
the Jews wished to draw out a clearcut answer, without any possible
equivocation: "Tell us whether thou art the Christ." [28] They
asked for an even surer guarantee: "Show us the Father, and it
is enough for us." [29] Certainly such a *proof* would be more than
sufficient; but proofs wound truth, and the Lord's refusal was
immediate and categorical: "Why does this generation demand a
sign? Amen I say to you, a sign shall not be given to this generation." [30]

[25] Eccles. 5, 1.
[26] Is. 63, 19.
[27] 2 Pet. 3, 4.
[28] Matt. 26, 13.
[29] John 14, 8.
[30] Mark 8, 12.

God has come, but it seems he does not want men to perceive his divinity. In the rare cases of his miracles, Jesus commanded: "Go and tell this to no man." Meditating, Pascal noted: "Revelation means that the veil has been removed; now the incarnation veils the face of God more." [31] God hides himself in his very manifestation, and this is the great mystery of the hidden God.

Reason, even at the moment when "all is consummated", lays down its conditions. "If he is the king of Israel, let him come down now from the cross, and we will believe him." [32] God answers by his silence, but for the one who knows how to listen, it is in this silence that "he declares his love to man".[33] This is the divine folly of which St. Paul speaks, the incomprehensible respect that God has for our freedom.

Every compelling proof violates the human conscience and changes faith into simple knowledge. That is why God limits his almighty power, encloses himself in the silence of his suffering love, withdraws all signs, suspends every miracle, casts a shadow over the brightness of his face. It is to this kenotic attitude of God that faith essentially responds. It keeps and will always keep an element of darkness, a crucifying obscurity, a sufficient margin to protect its freedom, in order to guard its power to say *no* at any moment and to build on this refusal. It is because a man can say *no* that his *yes* can attain a full resonance; his fiat is then not only in accord, but on the same dizzy level, of free creation as the fiat of God.

Faith is a dialogue, but the voice of God is almost silence. It exercises a pressure that is infinitely delicate and never irresistible. God does not give orders; he issues invitations: "Listen, Israel", or "If thou wouldst be perfect . . ." The decree of a tyrant is answered by a secret resistance; the invitation of the master of the banquet is answered by the joyful acceptance of the one "who has ears", who makes himself the chosen one by closing his hand on the gift offered.

More profoundly than the divine reserve in regard to man's

---

[31] *Lettre à Mile de Roannez* (Oct. 1656).
[32] Matt. 27, 42.
[33] Nicolas Cabasilas, *La Vie en Jésus-Christ.*

freedom, "the Lamb who has been slain from the foundation of
the world" ³⁴ indicates the ineffableness of the "suffering God".³⁵
In creating a "second freedom", God arouses a relation of reciprocity. The Father is father without imposing his fatherhood;
he offers himself in his Son, and every man is a son of God. "You
are gods," ³⁶ sons of the most high "gods" on the condition of
recognizing ourselves as sons in Christ and of saying with the
Holy Spirit: "Abba, Father." The freedom of sons is identified
and coincides with the gift of God, the Holy Spirit.

That is why God consents to be unappreciated, refused, rejected,
expelled from his own creation. On the cross, God took the part
of man against God.

The Christian is a miserable man, but he knows that there is
someone still more miserable, the beggar of love at the door of
man's heart. "Behold, I stand at the door and knock. If any man
listens to my voice, and opens the door to me, I will come in to
him and will sup with him, and he with me." ³⁷ The Son came
down to earth to sit at "the table of sinners".

From all eternity, God has thought only of the salvation of
man. Man ought to leave this care to God, and not seek for it
before all else; he ought even to forget it. He ought to think of the
salvation of divine love, for God has been the first to love; we do
not know why.

The attitude of God becomes clearer if we understand what is
mysterious about love—*all love is always reciprocal*. Love is possible only because it is miraculous, because it immediately engenders reciprocity, even if the latter is not conscious, refused or
perverted. This is why every great love is always a crucified love.
It produces a gift equal to its own grandeur, a royal gift because
it is free. In awaiting a fiat of equal vastness, love can only suffer
and be a pure oblation until death and the descent into hell.

John of Saroug, a Syrian writer, raises human love to the level

³⁴ Apoc. 13, 8.
³⁵ The expression is that of St. Gregory Nazianzen, who contemplates
the Lamb immolated *before* the incarnation, and who speaks with insistence
of the *passion* of the Being *impassible* by definition.
³⁶ John 10, 34.
³⁷ Apoc. 3, 20.

of Christ. "What man," he asks, "has ever died for his spouse, and what woman has ever chosen as her spouse one crucified? The Lord has espoused the Church, bestowed upon her a dowry by his blood, and forged for her a ring from the nails of his crucifixion." [38]

The sin of man is not disobedience. Disobedience is only an inevitable consequence of it. Sin is to repudiate the gift of communion, to refuse freedom, to give up filial love. God died that man may live in him. "It is now no longer I that live, but Christ lives in me." [39] Paul dies and Christ lives in him; this is the full development of the person of Paul, his entrance into the nuptial pleroma.

Science imposes its vision of visible and verifiable things and obliges me to accept them. I cannot deny an earthworm, nor a virus, but I can deny the existence of God. This is because faith, according to St. Paul, is "the evidence of things that are not seen".[40] It transcends the order of necessity. "Blessed are those who have not seen and who have believed" means blessed are those who are not compelled, forced, constrained.

Faith thus appears as a step beyond reason, commanded by reason itself when it reaches its limits. Faith says: "Give up your puny reason and receive the Word." It is a transcendence toward evidence, toward the hidden reality that reveals itself. It suppresses all demonstration, all intermediaries, all abstract notions of God, and it makes that someone who is the most intimately known immediately present.

The insufficiency of the proofs of God's existence is explained by a fundamental fact: God alone is the criterion of his truth, God alone is the argument of his being. In every thought concerning God, it is God who thinks himself in the human mind. That is why we can never prove his existence rationally nor convert another by arguments, for we can never do so in the place of God. We cannot submit God to the logic of demonstrations nor enclose him in a chain of causes.

[38] *Sur le voile de Moise,* quoted by Dom O. Rousseau in A. Raes, *Le Mariage dans les Eglises de l'Orient* (Chevetogne, 1958), p. 15.
[39] Gal. 2, 20.
[40] Heb. 11, 1.

If God is the sole argument of his existence, this means that faith is not invented. It is a gift, and it is to its royal and gratuitous nature that man must bear testimony, for faith is given to all in order that God may effect his Parousia in every human soul.

In accordance with his desires, the Word has chosen so strange a form that it constitutes a stumbling block. The Gospel is a chronicle of the life of Jesus, a collection of his words. However, there exist so many texts; there are the apocryphal gospels, the prophets of Pepuza, the wonderworkers and the messiahs even to our days. How can we choose?

The testimony of the apostles? Yes, but it is not absolutely convincing. It leaves a sufficient margin for doubts. There is a difference between a state of doubt and the difficulties of faith, but a thousand difficulties do not make a single doubt, as Newman said so profoundly. Historical criticism has dealt hard blows to all naive beliefs. There is a lack of irrefutable historic documents to prove even the earthly life of Jesus, without speaking of his heavenly life. This is very good; it is perhaps the best proof of the truth of the Gospel, for Jesus never imposed himself, never directly proclaimed his divinity. He asked only: "Do you believe this?" He never addressed himself to reason, never set forth proof or argument, never asked: "Do you know? Are you convinced? Are you conquered?" God's desires converge toward the heart in the biblical sense, and this focal point overthrows man's wisdom. Here the Holy Spirit rights the scales of justice and a careful man, like Job, weighs the proofs and the evidence, gives up the phantoms of doctrines and receives revelations. From this depth the words of St. Paul sprang forth: Nothing "will be able to separate us from the love of God, which is in Christ Jesus our Lord".[41] Here the famous paradox of Dostoievski is verified: "If one were to prove to me as a + b that truth is not on the side of Christ, I should remain on the side of Christ." This means that the truth that one proves as a + b can never be all the truth, that the truth of Christ is not commensurable with the truths of reason, that God is not only the object of faith but also the means which reveal him. The expressions, "the divine

[41] Rom. 8, 35.

eye", "the eyes of the dove", mean that it is God who looks at himself in us. Invisible to creatures, God is not invisible to himself, the Fathers say. "What is born of the Spirit is Spirit" means that man lives by the divine life. We see God by God, and it is this mystery that conditions and safeguards the mysteries of faith. God, affirms St. Gregory of Nyssa, remains always the "one sought for", the mysterious one. And St. Gregory of Nazianzen declares: "You have all names and how can I name you, you the only one that cannot be named?"

Man asks himself at least once in his life: "Where do I come from; where am I going?" This question is as old as the world. It seems that Christ had heard it when he said: "I come from the Father and I am going to the Father." This answer is repeated in the Creed. The symbol of faith, between the atheist's limitations and the agnostic's abdication, designates precisely the abyss of the Father.

Here the inspired argument of Dostoievski has its place. Man is defined by his Eros. "Where thy treasure is, there also will thy heart be." [42] If love, in the image of God, is the formula of man, it is evident that one can love only what is eternal. God and man are correlative, as Father and son. "The abyss of the heart aspires to the abyss of God." [43] "Thou hast made us for thyself, and our heart is restless until it rests in thee." [44] "It is in function of Christ that the human heart has been created; like an immense jewel case, it is vast enough to contain even God. That is why nothing here below can satisfy us. . . . For the human soul thirsts for the infinite . . . everything has been created for its end and the desire of the heart is to run toward Christ." [45]

"The light of Christ," says the office of Prime repeating St. John's prologue, "enlightens every man coming into the world."

[42] Matt. 6, 21.
[43] Angelus Silesius, cf. Ps. 42, 8: "An abyss calls to another abyss."
[44] St. Augustine, *Confessions*.
[45] Nicolas Cabasilas, *La Vie en Jésus-Christ*, translated by S. Broussaleux, p. 79.

Does there exist a single man to whom the faith has not been offered?

According to the Fathers, the Holy Spirit is the very essence of the gift of God. That is why there is one prayer that has never been refused, one which the Father always answers immediately, and that is the request for the Holy Spirit, the *epiklesis*. The man who seeks honestly and sincerely, who knows how to listen to the silence of his mind, can formulate the prayer of his heart in a conditional form: "If thou art, answer me, and send the Holy Spirit." "O God, if there is a God, enlighten me." Thus prayed a great Englishman who found both faith and an episcopal vocation. This is also the "if" of the inquiring and sincere Thomas to whom, however, it was given to say: "My Lord and my God!" Between the saddle and the ground, the rider may find grace, says an English proverb.

The Church cultivates the faith of martyrs and glorifies their confession: "It is thou whom I desire; in seeking thee, I struggle and I crucify myself with thee, in order to live in thee." [46] The martyr and confessor, the believer and the witness are synonymous. The *homologia* or proclamation is inherent in faith. Every believer tells what he has seen in God. He confesses publicly during the liturgy: "We have seen the true light; we have received the heavenly Spirit." He is a truthful eyewitness. From the depth of the eucharistic chalice, his faith can repeat the words of St. John: "I write . . . what we have heard, what we have looked upon and our hands have handled: of the Word of Life." [47] For faith, what is invisible is more intimate and better known than the visible. According to the beautiful words of Tauler: "Certain ones undergo martyrdom once by the sword; others know the martyrdom of love that crowns them interiorly," [48] invisibly for the world.

However, the confession of the martyrs is given to all in their last hour. In the face of the violence of death, the Credo resounds, and at the moment of death, it suppresses death. "Whether . . . life or

[46] Troparion of the virgin martyrs in the Greek liturgy.
[47] 1 John 1, 1.
[48] Quoted by Arnold, *La Femme dans l'Eglise* (Paris, 1955), p. 59.

death . . . all things are yours." [49] Thus even death is a gift, according to St. Paul. The believer is born, lives and dies in the miraculous, the permanent dimension of his faith.

God remains hidden, but he offers his saints and martyrs as "a spectacle" to men and angels. The pure of heart see God and by them God allows himself to be seen.

[49] 1 Cor. 3, 21.

3
Dimensions
of the Spiritual Life

The religious life of many believers is summed up in "religious practices": to assist at services, "to do his Easter duty", to fulfill his religious duties, without forgetting his philanthropic activities. Such a life is well filled, practical in many respects, and yet it risks having no connection with the spiritual life properly so-called. Even more, the common sense of the upright believer, set up as a reasonable system, can be like a formidable suit of armor through which can pass no folly, not even a miracle, or anything that could contrast with a man of the 20th century. Could he even catch the hidden irony in Pascal's wager instead of keeping a tranquil assurance from "supposing that . . ." ?

Moreover, persons exist who have an interior life that is very rich but not religious. Thinkers, artists, theosophists also, live an intense and profound psychic life, able to go as far as cosmic mysticism or spiritualism without God.

Therefore one can observe that of these two forms of life, "religious" and "interior", the first always entails a relation of dependence on a transcendent and personal absolute, and the second is autonomous and goes deep into the immanence of its own psychic richness.

The spiritual life alone integrates these two dimensions and shows them to be complementary. Essentially interior, it is also the life of man facing his God, participating in the life of God, the spirit of man listening for the Spirit of God.

Considered on the vaster plane of world religions, the spiritual life represents the Christian synthesis between the anthropocentric inwardness of the Oriental religions without God, and the transcendent and theocentric personalism of the biblical religions, Judaism

and Mohammedanism. In combining the marvelous penetration of
Hinduism into the abyss of human inwardness with the sacred fear
of Jewish and Mohammedan monotheism before the absolute
transcendence of the creator, the Christian, nevertheless, creates
an entirely new element. The divine *I* has spoken to a human *thou*.
His word has established the one who listens to him, has rendered
him existing in his image, and he continues to create and fill him
by keeping him in living communion with the *Word made flesh*.

The new tone of the Gospel is overwhelming. The God of the
Christians is most strange. He does not in any way resemble human
ideas concerning God, and this unheard of characteristic determines
the spiritual life. The creator of the world, in order to create it,
made himself "the lamb immolated since the beginning". And on
the cross, God took the part of man against his own deity. For
man's benefit, God is no longer all-powerful; he dies to himself
that man may live. He transcends his intra-divine silence toward
another *thee,* and introduces him into his mystery, into the sacred
circle of the trinitarian communion.

Since then man can say with St. Augustine: "You were at the
same time more inward than my inmost self and loftier than the
highest of myself." [50]

God desired to become man, and it is the incarnation that structures the divine and human nature of all spiritual life. In living it,
man is never alone; he lives it with God and God lives it in man
and with man. This participation of God in the human is decisive.
The spiritual life does not come from below, from human fabrication, from man's desires or from the longings of his soul. Man
does not invent it for his consolation. Such a romantic mythology
would never resist the trials of time and of death. The spiritual
life comes from above. God inaugurates it by the gift of his presence. Man receives this revelation-event and answers by his act of
faith. He formulates and confesses the Creed, the saying of the
Father's *thou* with his Son and his Spirit. A liturgical dialogue,
productive of unity, is begun.

[50] *Confessions,* III, vi, 11.

The spiritual life is an event in the interior of the spirit. Seen from the outside, it easily lends itself to misunderstandings and to frequent confusion with psychism. Thus psychologism formulates this classic question, which is beside the point, namely: "Does there exist a correspondence between the subjectivity of religious experience and the objectivity of its object?"

Thus propounded, the question prejudges its simplistic solution: the object of the experience—God—is only an aspect immanent in the soul, *esse in anima.* Man enters into dialogue with the elements of his own psyche, romanticizes them and makes them a mythology.

The error is to introduce a speculative distance between the experience and its object; *religious experience is at once the manifestation of its object.*

It is not a question of conformity between the experience and the spiritual reality, for the experience *is* this reality. The experience of the saints and mystics *is* the coming of the Spirit. The idea of God is not anthropomorphic. Man does not create God according to his own image; he does not invent him. However, the idea of man is theomorphic; God has created him in his image. Everything comes from God. The experience of God also comes from God because God is closer to man than man is to himself. As soon as God manifests his presence, man sees it. That is why nothing can be proved one way or another, but one who denies the reality of experience can at the most only prove that he has not lived it. The person of Christ is the place where once for all the experience of man by God and that of God by man have converged. It is this Christic reality that precedes every religious experience and actualizes it in Christ: "You are in me and I am in you." This reality interiorizes religious experience even to the point of divine intimacy.

One could almost say that the nuptial possession of man by God attains a kind of reciprocal substitution. The Holy Spirit utters in us and with us, as a single being: "Abba, Father." At his crucifixion Al Hallaj said: "I am the one whom I love and the one whom I love has become me." [51] "It is no longer I that

[51] See L. Massignon, *La passion d'Al Hallaj* (Paris, 1922).

live but Christ lives in me," St. Paul declared. Master Eckhart and Symeon the New Theologian describe in an identical manner this nuptial and eucharistic transmutation: "Thou becomest a single spirit with me, without confusion, without alteration." [52]

God cannot be made an object; consequently he is radically interior. "God is the more invisible the more his burning intimacy radiates in man's spirit." The spiritual life and religious experience are likewise incapable of being made objects. The very artificial psychological question, nevertheless, disturbs man and arouses a useless battle of words which is not fought on the level of evidence. It takes place on the exterior. Bergsonian intuitivism, in accordance with Oriental philosophy, permits us to affirm that every thought rendered too adequate to its verbal expression loses something of its dimension of depth. This is also the profound experience of L. Lavelle who wrote: "The word takes from the thought its purity and its secret"; on the other hand: "Silence does not differ at all from the inward word." [53] The more this interior thought-word matures in its silent depths the more it becomes inexpressible, ineffable. It is transformed into *evidence* that is all the more unprovable as it is irrefutable. The final logic of all revelation is evidence. The God of the Bible is before all else self-evident.

Another error is shown by syncretism. A psychologist easily crosses the frontiers of the various confessions, and he supposes that all religions converge. Nothing is comparable, however, to the truth of the Gospel offered and lived in the eucharist. It bears in Christ the accomplishment of the aspirations not only of men and angels, but of the three divine Persons, for according to Nicolas Cabasilas, the incarnation is the "pouring of God outside himself".

[52] *P.G.,* 120, col. 509.
[53] *La Parole et l'Ecriture,* pp. 133, 144.

4
The Dangers of Ignorance
and the Ascetic Art

In our day psychiatry recognizes that the origin of many organic illnesses lies in psychic disorders and in ignorance of the elementary principles governing the economy of the soul. Jung goes so far as to think that the fundamental problem of all the sick has its origin in the ambiguity of their religious attitude.[54]

The great uneasiness of modern man comes from his feeling a secret dependence on the elements he bears within the depths of his soul and which he no longer knows or understands, or which he fears to understand. Whether he is ignorant or not, it makes his psychic equilibrium very precarious and unstable. Although the rapid evolution of psychology has unsettled our knowledge of the human soul, this science has refused to define clearly the changing border between health and sickness.

How much more vulnerable is the man who is totally ignorant of his interior life. In moments of solitude or of suffering, he has no social formula to protect him or to solve the conflicts in his soul.

Freud saw in mental disorders a diversion or an escape from conflicts that had grown unbearable. In extreme cases, the instinct of self-preservation makes a man prefer madness to suicide.

Analysis does not stop at the level of the psyche. At a deeper level, psychiatrists who are believers discover spiritual disorders. For Jung, except in clinical cases, men suffer from the fact that their life is deprived of meaning and of any positive and creative content. Man is bored by his own indigence and is so worn out by his worries that, according to Jung: "His complexes very much resemble demons." This is the threshold of temptations, and ascetics know well the abyss of "sinful sadness" which ends in *acedia,* in dereliction or the extreme dejection of despondent souls.

Most believers, even when they are interested in psychology

54 *Die Beziehungen der Psychotherapie zur Seelsorge,* p. 16.

and know something about psychiatry or have submitted to it, manifest great levity in the spiritual life. Lived according to the inspiration of the moment and with a total lack of appreciation for its nature and its laws, the religious life of the the majority of believers fails since it offers only a feeble resistance to indifference and to the sensation of emptiness.

The simplifications of the positivists reduced sin to ignorance, crime to the influence of the social environment, evil to imperfection, and ascesis to hygiene. The notion of "sin" gets no hearing today; one does not know anymore what it means. According to the definition of the Sixth Ecumenical Council, *sin is a sickness of the spirit.* We know, on the other hand, that according to P. Janet: "Insanity is the loss of the function of the real." A madman no longer conceives reality as others do. Thus, not to be able to form an idea of sin and of its contrary, holiness, is a functional disorder, a form of spiritual madness.[55] When St. Paul asked for the spirit of discernment, he desired to find the norm, spiritual health, a function of total reality that comprises the earthly and the heavenly.

"Man," says Pascal, "is a mean between nothing and everything." He vacillates between nothingness and the absolute. The ambivalence of his situation leads to an acute sense of his own limits. Even when he has arrived at the summit of his genius, man remains like Job: "I cry for help but there is no redress."

At a certain level, this reflection borders on the pessimism that gnaws at the roots of life. Civilization is evolving and is causing a profound lack of equilibrium in the human mind; it is striking in its techniques and at the same time in the astonishing superficiality of its pragmatic philosophy. The universe is becoming a vast workshop where everything is expressed in figures and is submitted to the sole principle of production and curiosity. The anguish felt in the face of the inhuman anonymity of these enterprises provokes man to escapes that are in a rhythm more and more abrupt and jerky, the "atomic" style. The more the necessities of life weigh us down with all their constraints, the more does society tend to free itself from all taboos, and the general atmosphere to express a secret revolt. Is the modern world *for* or *against* man?

The biological rhythm of rural civilizations regulated by the sun

[55] "The fool says in his heart, 'There is no God'" (Ps. 13, 1).

gives way to the technical rhythm of invading and massive urbanization. Life in a world of factories and laboratories is no longer organic; it is organized. Its reinforced concrete very rapidly kills the sense of living nature. Even the simplest materials used in the administration of the sacraments—water, bread, wax, fire—are disappearing from natural use in homes, or are so falsified as to be no longer the familiar and known representation of the cosmos. Thus liturgical symbolism is not appreciated; the ritual no longer says anything spontaneously. It requires a very laborious initiation. The coming generations are more and more strangers to sacred symbols.

Modern symbolism takes refuge in insignia and groups of capital letters. Words are dehydrated and the most familiar objects seem to have lost their first meaning. We see in modern churches candles surmounted by an electric bulb, a hybrid which we do not know how to name.

Nevertheless, it is this world that is the object of God's care. He calls on Christian thought to make a creative effort and he asks it to translate into modern terms the immense heritage of the past, the precious experience of the great spiritual men of former times, all put in perfect harmony with the most venturesome life, thought and art.

It is not a question of modernism, but of a vision of what remains above time and by that fact directs history and man's destiny. It is on this level that the spiritual life can be offered again to wondering man, now become attentive to signs.

In present conditions, under the burden of overwork and the wear on nerves, sensibility is changing. Medicine protects and prolongs life, but at the same time it lowers resistance to suffering and privations. Christian ascesis is only a method in the service of life, and it will seek to adapt itself to the new needs. At Thebaid extreme fasts and constraints were imposed; today the combat is not the same. Man has no need of supplementary pain; hair shirts, chains, flagellations would run the risk of uselessly breaking him. Mortification could be the liberation from every kind of opiate— speed, noise, alcohol, and all kinds of stimulants. Rather, the ascesis could be necessary rest, the discipline of regular periods of calm and silence, when man could regain his ability to stop for prayer and contemplation, even in the heart of all the noises of the world; and he could then listen to the presence of others. The fast, as opposed to the maceration of the flesh inflicted on himself, could be his renunciation of the superfluous, his sharing with the poor and his smiling equilibrium.

The modalities of ascesis, like the faces of the saints, reflect the age. How symptomatic it is that in a world bowed down under the weight of cares, St. Thérèse speaks of spiritual childhood, traces her "little way", and invites all to sit down at "the table of sinners". Depth psychology for its part draws attention to the transcendence of humility and to the incarnations of the spiritual in social life. Modern ascesis sees itself in the service of the human that has been assumed in the incarnation; it is violently opposed to any lessening or abdication of man.

"No longer do I call you servants . . . . But I have called you friends." [56] These words of the Lord announce the adult state of man where man will go beyond man. The spiritual life is oriented toward divine friendship. The ascesis will divest itself of a penitential mentality and will become a preventive therapy. Almost everywhere monasticism seems to be seeking, beyond the somatic and psychological ascesis of the Middle Ages, the eschatological ascesis of the first centuries, that act of faith which kept the Christian in a joyful expectancy of the Parousia.

Experienced spiritual directors are rarer than ever; however, there is a vast ascetic literature that offers us a very precise knowledge of the human soul. If Freud and Jung professed their admiration for the psychological insight of Dostoievski, it was because he had been nourished by the works of the great spiritual writers.

From the time of Clement of Alexandria and Origen the spiritual bears the name of ascesis. This signifies application, training, exercise. The negative ascesis of suppression is allied to the positive ascesis of acquisition and growth of charisms. In a wide sense, an ascetic is a Christian who is mindful of the appeals of the Gospel, of the beatitudes, and who seeks humility and purity of heart in order to help his neighbor to do the same.

[56] John 15, 15.

5
Essential Elements
of the Spiritual Life

The word "spiritual" refers to the Holy Spirit and designates the level of being proper to "birth from on high", to "the nuptial mystery". It unveils the protophenomenon of every human person heedful of his heavenly origins.

Not only in history but also in the depths of the human soul Christ is born, dies and rises; baptism specifies this. It is in this inwardness that the bonds between God and man are forged and that the itinerary of the spiritual life is traced. The latter is always an encounter. God comes from himself toward man, and man leaves his solitude to meet his Other. "Never have you disdained anyone, and it is we, on the contrary, who hide ourselves, not wanting to go to you," said St. Symeon.

Thus, the constitutive elements of the spiritual life go beyond the human. Dante speaks of the three partners in the divine game —God, man, and Satan. The ascetic specifies the three wills that confront one another: (1) that of God, salvific and working within man under the form of appeals and invitations, and this is *theonomy;* man may adhere to it and make it his own; (2) that of man, unstable and uncertain; it is his *autonomy* that encloses himself within himself; (3) finally there is that of Satan, hostile to man, and which makes him come out of himself without preparing any encounter for him; this is *heteronomy*—submission, slavery, perdition.

There is very little to say on the *divine element* in the spiritual life. It is more proper to be silent and to venerate it in silence. God is the initiator, and in his presence he is radically transcendent. "Flesh and blood have not revealed this to you, but my Father in

49

heaven," [57] "and that not from yourselves, for it is a gift of God," [58] it is a gratuitous gift. By his love alone, God makes of man his trinitarian abode. "We will come to him and make our abode with him." [59] This act in its incomparable grandeur has no common measure with human effort; the three divine persons dwell in the soul according to man's capacity to receive them.

A contemporary spiritual writer admirably expresses this idea. "God gives himself to men according to their thirst; to certain ones, who could not drink any more, he gives only a drop; but he would love to give great draughts in order that Christians could in their turn quench the world's thirst." [60]

It is evident that on this level of the divine initiative, there is no technique or method of the spiritual life. Grace grants its gifts and man is only a receptacle, though with the angels astounded and plunged in deep wonder.

The *demoniac* element represents the obstacle. "He was a murderer from the beginning, and has not stood in the truth." [61] This adversary wages an uninterrupted struggle. "Be watchful. For your adversary the devil, as a roaring lion, goes about seeking someone to devour." [62] "Put on the armor of God, that you may be able to stand against the wiles of the devil." [63]

It is on this plane of struggle that man is an active agent. This technique, this very refined strategy of "the invisible fight" constitutes the ascesis.

Finally, there is the *human* element aspiring to lift itself beyond all struggle. It is expressed essentially in the liturgical attitude of adoration. "I will sing to the Lord all my life." [64]

An anonymous mystic of the Middle Ages has expressed it in humble but beautiful words: "I am an ass, but I carry my Lord."

"Behold, I stand at the door and knock. If any man listens to

[57] Matt. 16, 17.
[58] Eph. 2, 8.
[59] John 14, 23.
[60] *Revue Contacts*, nn. 35-36, p. 248.
[61] John 8, 44.
[62] 1 Pet. 5, 8.
[63] Eph. 6, 11.
[64] Ps. 103, 33.

my voice and opens the door to me, I will come in to him and will sup with him, and he with me." [65] The initiative of God who knocks is answered by the eagerness of the human being who keeps himself in readiness for this event. He hears and opens the door of his soul, prostrates himself before his visitor, and sits down with him at the banquet. The Fathers loved to comment on the parable of the prodigal son, which puts into relief the decision, the act that places the human action within the divine action. "When he came to himself, he said . . . 'I will get up and go to my father. . . .' And he arose and went to his father." [66]

According to St. Cyril, it is this decision that makes the man who is invited one of the chosen, and this is precisely the creative effort of positive asceticism. If it is not commenced at the very beginning, St. Macarius teaches, if it does not precede negative, normative and disciplinary asceticism, the latter is of no use.

On the eve of Lent, a wise saying warns: "The devil does not eat, he does not drink, and he does not marry, and this great ascetic formally is not less a devil . . . " "Let us always relate the non-essentials—fast, watchings, solitude—to the principal end, the purity of heart that is charity," [67] as Cassian teaches in quoting Abbot Moses.

[65] Apoc. 3, 20.
[66] Luke 15, 17-20.
[67] *Confessions*, I.

6
The Nature or Essence
of the Spiritual Life

"In the beginning", at the time of the decisive testing of man, the resounding failure of his choice made him fall *below* the level of his being and immersed him in the life of the senses and of matter. Man became carnally and sensually enveloped in darkness, but the economy of salvation lifted him *above* the level of his being even to that of a *new creature*. St. Paul's dialectic here takes its point of departure. "Even though our outer man is decaying, yet our inner man is being renewed day by day." [68] "Strip off the old man . . . and put on the new." [69]

The spiritual life is oriented toward this metamorphosis, "to put on the new man". What makes the man new is the fact that he is no longer alone. More profoundly and at the heart of his transmutation, he is the man who has "put on Christ", he is a Christlike man.

The Fathers take almost literally the fact of putting on Christ and see in it a projection or, more exactly, a prolongation in man of the incarnation of the Word, perpetuated especially in the eucharist. That is why they teach us not to "imitate" but interiorize him. This inwardness is not a simple metaphor which would force the meaning; it has its roots deep in God himself. If the incarnation reflects a certain anthropomorphism of God (a mysterious primordial conformity), it reveals above all and assuredly the *theomorphosis* of man. From the biblical point of view, the incarnation brings to perfection our nature, which is made to the image of God, and it reveals the manifestly Christological structure of the spiritual life.

Man then traverses an immense distance to the interior of his

[68] 2 Cor. 4, 16.
[69] Col. 3, 9-10.

being. St. Paul quotes a primitive hymn charged with almost explosive dynamism. "Awake, sleeper, and arise from among the dead, and Christ will enlighten you." [70] A variant reinforces its meaning: "You will touch Christ." This passage from the state of death to the state of life, from hell to the kingdom, is precisely the itinerary of the spiritual life.

Moralizing spirituality reduces salvation to the forgiveness of disobedience. Now biblical ontology, vigorous and exacting, leads from a moral catharsis (purification) to an ontological catharsis. This represents a very real change in the whole human being— body, soul and mind. It is the strongest affirmation of patristic exegesis, stressing the Gospel's call to metanoia or conversion. "Repent, for the kingdom of heaven is at hand." [71] It would be more exact to say: "Change yourself", become a new creature, for it is a question of a repentance in the full meaning of the word— a complete turning about of the mind and of the whole human being.

The encounter with God could not be effected in the state of fallen nature; it presupposes a previous restoration of this nature in the sacrament of baptism. For baptism, according to the Fathers, is a true re-creation of the redeemed man. Repentance, metanoia in its complete meaning, goes to the roots of all mental faculties, volitional and affective, and even to the heart of the entire being, body and soul. St. Irenaeus, in his celebrated doctrine of the recapitulation of all nature in Christ, closely follows St. Paul. St. John's Gospel emphasizes it in speaking of the "second birth". The two terms, metanoia and birth, express clearly that profound modification of the human being and mark its entrance into the spiritual world, whose principles are the opposite of those of the world. Between a baptized and an unbaptized person there is the abyss of the infinite difference of the two natures. To stress this absolutely new character, the Fathers chose by preference the miracle of the wedding feast of Cana. The symbolism of this image makes baptism and the eucharist converge. In fact, the baptismal water has the value of the blood of Christ, declares Nicolas Cabasilas: "It

---

[70] Eph. 5, 14.
[71] Matt. 3, 2.

destroys a life and produces another . . . we leave our tunics of leather to put on a kingly mantle." [72]

We can now understand how the spiritual life at once effects a *break*. It is not the same life as before with the addition of some religious service, reading and pious attitudes. It is essentially a break, a combat, a violence that takes heaven by assault and seizes the kingdom. On the threshold of this life resounds the words of St. Paul: "Behold, they are made new." [73]

The Gospel mentions the formidable power of the prince of this world. St. Paul, in calling him "god of this world",[74] emphasizes the state of alienation of man by the diabolic powers, and it is this power of Satan which requires a complete break. We find it in the very expressive symbolism of baptism; the total immersion signifies real death to a guilty past, and emersion, the definitive victory, the resurrection to a new life. The "promise" of baptism, however, the great baptismal profession of faith in the Trinity, presupposes a radical intervention of purification and a personal act of the human being. Indeed, the Church takes very seriously the power of evil and its murderous ravages. This is why the ancient rites placed before baptism the *lavacrum,* the rite of exorcism and of solemn renouncing of the evil one.

The priest reproduces the divine act; he breathes on the face of the "dead" the breath of life, analogous to the breathing of life into man when he was created. Facing the West, the kingdom of the prince of this world, where the light of day disappears, the neophyte renounces his past that had been placed under the power of the enemy. Miming symbolically the struggle he must sustain all the length of his spiritual life, he turns toward the East, where day appears, and confesses his faith and receives grace.

This ritual contains in germ the essence of his new existence. Negatively, it is incessant combat; positively, it is the metamorphosis asked for in the final baptismal prayer with its Pauline accents: "O God, divest him of the old man, renew him and fill him with the power of your Holy Spirit, in the union of Christ."

[72] N. Cabasilas, *op. cit.,* p. 52.
[73] 2 Cor. 5, 17.
[74] 2 Cor. 4, 4.

This is a very compact summary of the spiritual life; its progression never stops. "No one, having put his hand to the plough
and looking back, is fit for the kingdom of God." [75] Every halt is a
regression. The total character of the consecration of every baptized
and confirmed person, stressed in the rite of tonsure, places him in
the extreme tension of every instant, in his yearning for the ultimate,
the impossible. This rite of tonsure, an organic part of the sacrament of confirmation in the Oriental Church, is identical to that
undergone when one enters a monastic order. The prayer of the
ritual asks: "Bless your servant who has come to give you as his
first offering the tonsure of the hair of his head." Its symbolic
meaning is very clear, it is the total offering of his life. In undergoing the rite of tonsure, every lay person finds himself a monk of
"interior monasticism", submissive to all the absolute exigencies of
the Gospel. The fidelity of the neophyte is going to resist the trials
of time and the assault of temptations, for Christ is going to fight
in him and with him.

[75] Luke 9, 62.

7
The Different Ages
of the Spiritual Life

Poets sing of the marvel of a glance that is always unique. The destiny of each one also seems unique. There exists, however, a certain correspondence between the phases of each spiritual life as in the rhythm of different ages. An element remains constant, around which the destiny of each human life is formed. The circumstances change, but the spiritual theme, personal for each one, remains identical through all disguises. Its call and the unavoidable exigency of an answer, this combination of what is given and what is desired, constitute what the Gospel calls the personal cross of each man. It is inscribed within us at birth; no power can change it. "Which of you by being anxious about it can add to his stature a single cubit?" [76]

Whether in the heart of a great city or in the midst of a desert, we cannot flee from this personal theme of our life. It accompanies us and speaks to us at every turning on our road. We can answer differently and each time change our course in one direction or another. We can marry or become monks; we can, like Spinoza, polish lenses or repair shoes like Jacob Boehme. The question, our question, remains identical and fixed in us as a constituent element of our being; it is no longer a question, it is we ourselves who are involved.

To understand our "cross" is to foresee the facts of our destiny, to decipher its meaning; it is to understand ourselves. The spiritual life does this; it introduces order, reveals the rhythm of its own growth, and requires a progressive advance.

Religious psychology traces the outline of the evolution in three periods: (1) the preliminary unity of the human being; this is

[76] Matt. 6, 27.

57

precarious and unstable; (2) the sharp conflict between the spiritual and the empiric; (3) and at the last, the final integration.

With rare exceptions, the spiritual life comes into being in an event that is called "conversion". Its precise content is of little importance; it is a notable occasion, a shock followed by a sharply defined passage from one state to another. Just as light reveals shadows, it suddenly unveils the inadequacy of the unstable present and orients us to doors opening upon a new world. This beginning of an untried promise causes decisive actions and entails the joyful commitment of our whole being. Even those who have inherited the faith in their childhood pass sooner or later through this by a conscious discovery of their faith, and by appropriating it to themselves personally; this is always an overwhelming experience.

A reading, a meeting, a reflection causes a sudden light to break forth brilliantly. In its brightness, all is seen in its right order as in an inspired poem that gives to each thing a new and inestimable value. It is a religious springtime, full of joyousness and enthusiasm. Like the buds filled with sap, the human being feels himself dilated by a surprising joy and a spontaneous sympathy for everything. This is an unforgettable time. Like a feast illuminated by a thousand lights, it makes one see in God the smiling countenance of the Father coming to meet his child.

This time is of short duration. The face of the Father takes on the face of the Son, and his cross casts its shadow within us. Our own cross stands out clearly, and there is no possible return to the simple and childlike faith of former days. Sorrowful discords tear our soul in its clearsighted vision of evil and sin; it is an extreme tension between two states that are mutually exclusive. The brutal experience of our falls and weakness can fling us to the edge of despair. We are strongly tempted to cry out that it is an injustice, that God expects too much from us, that our cross is heavier than that of others. An old story tells of a simple and sincere man who felt a similar revolt. An angel led him to a pile of crosses of different sizes and told him to choose. The man chose the lightest, and at once discovered that it was his own! We are never tempted beyond our strength.

God is watching us at the decisive moment. He expects from

our faith a vigorous act, the full and conscious acceptance of our destiny; he asks us to assume it freely. No one can do it in our place, not even God himself. The cross is made of our weaknesses and our failings; it is constructed by our enthusiastic impulses and especially by the dark depths of our heart where a secret resistance and a shameful ugliness lurk, by all that complexity which is at this precise moment, the authentic *I*.

"Love your neighbor as yourself," allows a certain love of self. It is a call to love our cross. It means perhaps the most difficult act of all—to accept ourselves as we are. We know that the proudest beings, those most avid of self-love, are those who feel ill at ease with themselves and who secretly hate themselves. It is an infinitely serious moment when one encounters himself, for this requires a baring of himself, an immediate and total vision of himself even in his most secret recesses.

"He who sees himself as he is, is greater than the one who raises the dead," [77] spiritual men say, stressing thus the importance of this act. The vision is always frightening; consequently we must contemplate Christ. This is the experience of St. Paul and of every Christian. "When I wish to do good, I discover this law, namely, that evil is at hand for me . . . Unhappy man that I am! Who will deliver me from the body of this death? . . . Jesus Christ, our Lord." [78]

In moments of crushing solitude, humility alone can help us in recognizing the radical powerlessness of human nature. It inclines us to cast our whole being at the foot of the cross, and then our heavy burden is lifted by Christ in our place: "Learn of me . . . . For my yoke is easy, and my burden light." [79]

"Thy will be done," the fiat springs forth; I accept is as my own. I read in it what God has thought of me, and I recognize my destiny. We are no longer self-centered, but rendered joyful and lighthearted. "Behold the handmaid of the Lord." [80] "The friend of the bridegroom, who stands and hears him, rejoices exceedingly

[77] St. Isaac the Syrian, *Sentences.*
[78] Rom. 7, 21-24.
[79] Matt. 11, 29-30.
[80] Luke 1, 38.

at the voice of the bridegroom. This my joy, therefore, is made full." [81]

According to spiritual writers, the art of humility does not consist of becoming this or that, but of being in the exact measure proposed by God. Dostoievski describes this vivid moment by the mouth of the pilgrim Macarius in *The Adolescent*. With a single glance, this man envelops the universe, his life, time and eternity. He can only say as a final chord, "All is in you, Lord; I am yours; receive me." Without being yet able to understand everything, man seizes more than he needs at the moment. His destiny finds the freshness of a passionately loved existence. It is only after this "second birth", this personal Pentecost, that the spiritual life properly so-called begins.

[81] John 3, 29.

II

THE OBSTACLE AND THE STRUGGLE

1
Negations of Evil and
Affirmations of Good

In Greek the words "symbol" and "devil" come from the same root, and thus they express more forcefully two contrary realities. The devil is a divider, one who separates and cuts off all communication, reducing a being to the utmost solitude. On the other hand, a symbol binds together, builds a bridge, reestablishes communion.

The story of the possessed man of Gerasa [1] shows clearly the nature of evil. Christ asked the devil a formidable question: "What is thy name?" For the Jewish mentality the name of an object or a being expresses its essence, and the old adage, "nomen est omen", sees in the name the expression of a person and his destiny. Christ's question meant therefore: "Who are you; what is your destiny, your secret being?" The demon answered: "*My* name is legion, for *we* are many."

This brusque transition from *my* to *we* reveals the action of evil in the world. The innocent being created by God is broken, splintered into isolated particles, and this is hell. Both the Greek *Hades* and the Hebrew *Sheol* mean that dark place where solitude reduces a being to the extreme indigence of demoniacal solipsism. We can represent hell as a cage made of mirrors; one can see in them only one's own face multiplied to infinity, without a glimpse of anyone else's. To see only oneself is to be satiated with oneself even to the point of nausea, even to the ontological hiccup. The coptic *Apophtegms* of Macarius the Ancient give a striking description of this solitude. The captives are tied to one another by their backs, and only a strong prayer uttered by the living can bring

[1] Mark 5, 9.

63

them an instant of rest. "For the time of a twinkling of an eye, we see one another's faces."

On the contrary, confronted with this action of evil, St. Paul [2] shows us the action of good, of Christ: "Because the bread is one (Christ), we though many, are one body, all of us who partake of the one bread." [3] In the eucharistic communion we find the *one* of all who are recapitulated in Christ in the image of the trinitarian communion, God who is one and at the same time three, unity in multiplicity.

It is natural then that the eucharist has its place in the very center of the Church and reveals itself as productive of the unity that is proclaimed, offered and lived. Like a golden block without the least fissure, it constitutes the *esse* of the Church. The most ancient invocation, *Marana tha* (Come, Lord),[4] completes a liturgical prayer and refers to the Parousia, to the eucharistic coming of the risen Lord.[5] God comes to offer himself as nourishment, and we consume his substance, the agape, "incorruptible love".[6] Eucharistic communion effects a substantial participation in the total Christ, and this work, unitive by essence, makes the communicants, according to St. Athanasius, beings that "have been made like the Word, Christified". St. Ignatius of Antioch sees in the eucharist a "remedy of immortality", that cures death.[7] Even more, in consuming the flesh and blood of the spouse, we enter into a nuptial *koinonia* (communion), says St. Theodore of Cyr.[8] This communion fills us to such an extent that one "can go no further nor add anything".[9]

The *henosis,* "the one with Christ", lived in the eucharist, determines *the eucharistic style of the spiritual life.* Communion accomplished with Christ and his body—men—becomes an entirely

[2] 1 Cor. 10, 17; 12, 12.

[3] Cf. Rom. 12, 5. The apostle here repeats the devil's expression; the being decomposed by evil into many, into a legion, a wicked multitude.

[4] 1 Cor. 16, 22; Apoc. 22, 20; the *Didache,* chapter 16.

[5] See O. Cullmann, *Le Culte dans l'Eglise primitive* (Paris, 1945).

[6] St. Ignatius of Antioch, Rom. 7, 2; Eph. 14, 1.

[7] Eph. 13.

[8] See J. Daniélou, *Eucharistie et Cantique des Cantiques* (Irenikon, 1950), p. 275.

[9] N. Cabasilas, *op. cit.,* p. 97.

positive growth: "Between the body and the head, there is no room for any interval, for any negation." [10] All who participate in God "in whom there is only *yes*", profess an entire *yes* to life, to being. On the other hand, there is only *no* in Satan, and this refusal marks the limits of the place from which God is excluded, negation, nothingness, hell.

St. John [11] recognizes this *no* in sin that signifies transgression, going beyond the ontological limits set by God and traced by his name: "I am the one who is." The third prayer of the *Didache* speaks of it: "We give you thanks, O Holy Father, for your holy name that you have caused to dwell in our hearts. It is you, almighty master, who have created the universe in your name." [12] "I am a great king, says the Lord, my name is adorable among all the nations." [13] To go beyond this limit is to break the original bond, to renounce the king, to claim autonomy and to place oneself outside the name.

Atheism suppresses this limit of created being in its radical denial of all dependency. In place of the human thirst for "the wholly other", it substitutes the decision to live "as if" this limit had been rendered forever non-existent. Such is Western atheism. The atheism of the anti-God militants of the Soviet world is, in a certain sense, more consistent and radical. Faithful to the historic interest inherent in Russian thought (Tchaadaeff, Berdyaev), it is centered in only one negation since this is *historic:* "Christ has not risen."

It is fitting to mention here the name of St. Isaac the Syrian. Living in the 7th century, he made a synthesis of patristic thought, and as a master of ascesis, wrote a phenomenology of sin. Without attaching much importance to the multitude of sins which are almost small, one might say, in the sight of God since he forgives them, Isaac points out in his *Sentences* the unique sin, *the* sin, which is *to be insensible to the resurrection!* A moving prophecy of the Soviet atheism of today. To be efficacious, it attacks only the ir-

---

[10] St. John Chrysostom, *P.G.*, 62, 26.
[11] 1 John 3, 4.
[12] X, 2.
[13] XIV.

refutable argument of the cross, and this is a question not of man alone, but of God. Indeed the denial of the resurrection attacks, beyond the creative act, the Creator himself. Mystically this denial effects deicide, the murder of the Father. Nietzsche had formulated it well in speaking of the death of God. "Where is God? I am going to tell you. We have killed him." The conscience of atheists culminates there, according to Dostoievski: "There was once on earth a day when three crosses were lifted up in the center of the world . . . toward the end of the day they died . . . but they found neither paradise nor resurrection . . . That is the idea, the whole idea. Outside it, there is no other." [14] This is the very heart of atheism. It is the secret source from which comes the Freudian complex of universal guilt—the death of the Father—and the inclination of a being toward death, *Todestrieb,* and likewise Heidegger's formula, *Sein zum Tode.*

"*Alea jacta est*": the die is cast, the choice is made, the atheist's Credo is proclaimed *orbi et urbi:* God is dead and he does not arise. "The lamb slain from the foundations of the world" means the lamb immolated and truly dead, annihilated, non-existent. In the beginning there was the death of God and his silence.

Since his destiny is at stake, man is driven to choose between the alternatives of *yes* and *no;* there is no third choice. Nietzsche expressed this in his correspondence. There are two follies, he says, that make men live; one is the one he chose, the folly of the superman, surviving in the eternal return; the other, which to him was unacceptable, is that of St. Paul, the folly of the cross, of the risen God and of immortal man.

The atheistic argument was foreseen by St. Paul.[15] If Christ is not risen, our faith is vain, nothing has meaning, and all is nothingness. There are no half measures, no intermediary formulas. We are in the presence of the fundamental evidence of Jesus risen from the dead. A God who does not present his charter as lover of mankind, a God who is not love crucified in order to radiate "life, death of death", as St. Augustine says, is not really God. In following St. Paul's thought to its conclusion, we could say that all religion

14 *The Possessed.*
15 1 Cor. 15, 14.

exists only by the resurrection and mystically leans on this event. If Christ is risen, this is of interest for all men. If the Christian testimony to the risen Lord is suppressed, no religion will survive on the level of the modern world, for outside the Gospel every religious message stops halfway.

The Gospel's transcendent end is God become a risen *Man*. This fact does not concern just a few witnesses only; the risen Christ in becoming the contemporary of all men means that every man is *contemporary with the eternal Christ*. This makes all the events of history essentially christological. Christ is risen as head of the human body, and now all religions and all men can and ought to seek their life in him. This testimony alone determines the ecumenical mission of the Church in the midst of all religions and in the great meeting between East and West. History places the Christian faith in the risen Christ at the crossing point of all ideologies that now reformulate the only important question—that asked by Pilate—"What is truth?" It obliges faith to say its *yes,* going if need be as far as the confession of martyrdom, that unique answer that resounds universally. Christ is in agony, and eternity is impatient to hear this answer.

The apostolic kerygma announces the event of Easter, the intervention of God raising up Jesus; this alone gives a definitive meaning to the existence of men in history. We find its central core in 1 Corinthians 15, 3-4, in Romans 4, 24-25 and Acts 2, 36. The resurrection of Jesus is God's amen to his promise, an amen full of the Holy Spirit who manifests it. Amen comes from the Hebrew *heemin* and it means an unshakable base of operations. Those who proclaim it—the apostles and martyrs—claim the right to proclaim the event before the magistrates of the earthly city. Likewise the Apologies of Justin, Athenagoras, and Aristides present to emperors the same decisive message and warn them of the imminent judgment. Their kerygma is of interest to all men. It is preached in the presence of angels and concerns all of creation: the kingdom of God has already arrived; we are contemporaries of the one who sits at the right hand of the Father. Here is the lamb immolated and risen and here is his kingdom. He is here and it is the fullness of time. All religions are ways by which men seek God. They are

numerous. However, the Christian revelation is unique for it is God
who finds man. The preaching of St. Paul is of capital importance
for the theology of religion. In deciphering the monument to the
unknown God and in giving it the name, Jesus Christ, the apostle
integrated with Christ the religious aspiration of all times and gave
it value in Christ.

Man's transgression confines him to a situation that is closed to
all that is not of this earth. The more material this is and the more
it is made a thing, the more it appears deprived of reality and of
any substance. This is the world of finance, with its temple, the
Stock Exchange, and its votaries of luxury; it is the political world
of ambition and covetousness, of collective neurosis of mad passions and unfaithful sensual love. It is a world vacillating above an
abyss, without any consistency, being made of vapors and peopled
with phantoms, and which at any moment risks disappearing "as
smoke in the air and as wax melted by fire". On the other hand,
Origen compares the efforts of the hermits of the desert, in their
march toward perfection,[16] to the slow departure of the inhabitants
of Plato's cave. Leaving the silhouetted shadows for a vision of
reality, where nothing is interposed between man and the truths of
the divine life, the monk of the desert kept firmly to the way
of return toward the kingdom.

We find a vigorous and complete vision of human destiny even
in the beginnings of Christian thought. St. Gregory of Nyssa [17]
mentions the celebrated catechism of the *two ways. The Testament
of XII Patriarchs* clearly formulates it: "God has given two ways
to the son of man and two inclinations, and two manners of acting,
and two ends." This is the doctrine of the two *yeser,* of the two
inclinations of the heart, in conformity either to the action of the
angel of light or to the action of the angel of darkness. The
Didache, the *Epistle of Barnabas,* and other writings draw from the
same source, and this theme was to have a great influence on Christian letters. It goes back to the option offered by God, "I have

[16] A group of ascetics used to be designated by the name of *synodia* or
caravan.
[17] *Life of Moses,* II, 45.

set before you life and death." [18] It is always the same choice between *yes* and *no*.

According to the Bible, the fool is free to say in his heart: "There is no God." However, the meaning of the negation changes according to the level of depth and suffering in the one who denies. That is why *"Perfect atheism* (perfect here means lived even to suffering) is at the top of the ladder, on the second last step before perfect faith," as Dostoievski affirms.[19] When, far from formless indifference, atheism and faith are carried to "perfection", they can meet together above senseless talk, in the silent combat of the angel with Jacob, and of grace with despair. Consistent atheism, burning with suffering, knows its own paradoxical cross. At the end of his life, on notes scribbled at the height of his madness, Nietzsche wrote his definitive name—the Crucified. Likewise the atheistic Great Inquisitor [20] made fun of materialism and positivism, but he attained his true grandeur in his passion for man. His *no,* in spite of himself, would almost participate in the love of God for man, though he is not conscious of this. Perhaps passion for man goes beyond a certain level that is merely human. Is not the essence of the divine heart this same passion, and would there not be here one of those mysterious "passages to the limit"? Perhaps it is necessary to be a saintly "philanthropist", in the manner of God, in order to feel the deep correspondence. There exists a purifying atheism, according to the words of Jules Lagneau, "that salt which hinders belief in God from corrupting itself". In this function of protection and safeguard, it cooperated with grace. That is why the Christ of the *Legend* of Dostoievski is silent, and kisses the face of the Great Inquisitor contracted with suffering.

[18] Deut. 30, 19.
[19] "Confession of Stavrogin," in *The Possessed.*
[20] *The Brothers Karamazov.*

2
Three Aspects of Evil
and the Evil One

Among the multiple manifestations of evil, one can discern three symptomatic aspects—parasitism, imposture and parody. The evil one lives as a parasite on the being created by God, forming a monstrous excrescence, a demoniacal swelling. An imposter, he covets the divine attributes, and substitutes equality for resemblance. "You will be as God", as his equals. Finally, as a jealous counterfeiter, he imitates the creator and constructs his own kingdom without God, an imitation with an inverse sign.

The philosophers have never succeeded in elucidating the problem of evil; they have rather complicated and entangled it. Evil, on the contrary, was never a problem for the Fathers of the Church. For them it was not a question of speculating on evil, but rather of fighting the evil one. The prayer of a saint would be: "Preserve us from all vain speculation on evil and deliver us from the evil one." Likewise, the Bible does not speak of ethical principles concerning good and evil but it reveals God and mentions the adversary; it denounces also "the man of iniquity of the last days", "the son of perdition who . . . gives himself out as if he were God".[21]

From the very heart of his being the devil "from the beginning" has been a murderer, according to the words of Christ.[22] A spirit of negation, he is above all a murderer of his own truth, that of being Lucifer, a receptacle of divine light. Thus, he consummates his own metaphysical *suicide,* and sets himself up in universal denial of the imprint of God. He thus attains at the same time *homicide* and *deicide.*

[21] 2 Thess. 2, 3-4.
[22] John 8, 44.

If for Plato the contrary of truth is error, at the deeper level of the Gospel, it is the lie. "Liar and father of lies" by essence, the evil one has taken upon himself a frightful vocation, that of knowingly altering truth. The initial perversion of his will has made it possible for him to usurp whatever he can in order to fabricate an existence with spurious materials. Isaiah clearly designates this enterprise: "We have made lies our refuge, and in falsehood we have found a hiding place." [23]

To lie in the face of heaven is to oppose God's truth and to impose one's own version on the world. The devil sets himself up as a counterpart in order to dislodge God from his creation, which he tries to make insensible to the divine presence, and thus to effect a gigantic substitution. Disdainfully proud, he says: "I, and no one else", "A god am I." [24]

"When he tells a lie, he speaks from his very nature." [25] This judgment of the Lord contains a whole philosophy of evil. Every lie by its nature originates in what is false, that is to say, the nonexisting. The "very nature" of the evil one, from where he draws his lies, is then nothingness. Thus St. Gregory of Nyssa could define evil as having a phantom-like substance. God, by his fiat—his *yes* —creates similarities and completely fills all beings. The evil one, by his *no*—his anti-fiat—expels and completely empties all, and he constitutes "a place of dissimilarity".[26] On the other hand, "the saints are those who do not speak from their own nature, but it is God" [27] who speaks in them, and they thus form "the place of similarity". The dreadful secret of Satan conceals the absence of any metaphysical foundation, and this emptiness obliges him to borrow, to usurp, the being founded and rooted in the creative act of God. Evil, as a parasite, sticks to being, vampirizes and devours it.

The Scriptures do not teach philosophy. The Bible does not see

[23] Is. 28, 15.
[24] Ezek. 28, 2; Is. 47, 8.
[25] John 8, 44. The Samaritan code in Gen. 3, 2 in place of "serpent" reads *the liar*, which puts it in harmony with John 8, 44.
[26] See L. Ouspensky, *Essai sur la théologie de l'icone* (Paris, 1960), p. 187, note 1.
[27] Barsanuphius, *Lettres*, 885.

in evil a simple lack of good or of perfection, a non-plenitude, but a liberty that has failed and has turned into an evil will. In adding the non-existent to the existent, it has perverted this into a malevolent being. However, this perversion, or evil, is not materialized and personalized in the evil one except under certain conditions; men must furnish him with ontological "board and lodging" which means that, thanks to their freedom, men can be conscious or unconscious accomplices in serving a lie. In this real ministry of those "possessed" by evil, beings are diminished so that the Liar may swell and grow. His tragedy is that the nourishment of the gods, "the bread of the mighty (angels) . . . eaten by men",[28] is lacking to the devil, for the heavenly wheat is the accomplishment of the Father's will. This will is the substance of all things, St. Irenaeus teaches. Thus in the world of God, the phantom-like evil one, famished for the real, is a metaphysical "sponger". He feasts on the seizure of men, and his horrible carousals, by increasing the emptiness caused by the absence of God, are for them the beginning of hell here below.

Where there is no God there is no man either. The loss of the image of God entails the disappearance of man's image, dehumanizes the world, and multiplies "the possessed". The absence of God is replaced by the burdensome presence of one obsessed by himself, a self-idol;[29] in the long run his sad utopias risk modifying our anthropological type. Man loses his dimension of depth, the dimension of the Holy Spirit. According to the bold words of St. Gregory of Nyssa, one who is not moved by the Holy Spirit is not a human being.

Every passion bears within it the seed of death since it dulls the spirit of discernment. Likewise every bad means is never justified by a good end for it is already its negation. One can say just the contrary; the good means to a bad end runs the risk of changing into good. It is entirely a question of foundation and of source. Temptations never come up to the expectations they arouse, for evil possesses no source of life within it; it satiates without ever satisfying or quenching thirst. It is not in its power to repeat the

[28] Ps. 77, 25.
[29] St. Andrew of Crete, the *Canon* read during Lent.

words of the Lord: "Who drinks of the water that I will give him shall never thirst."[30] The one who seeks other springs imposes on himself unquenchable thirsts.

At the bottom of every state of passion, whether it be ambition, eroticism, gambling or narcotics, there is a simple mechanism of possession which, once broken, strikes us by the dullness of its meager content conducive to boredom. As the oyster secretes its shell, every ideology which makes atheism its passion ends sooner or later by secreting boredom. Shrewd observers remark this symptomatic state of soul. It is especially true of the ponderous gravity of the doctrinaires, busy in making "the new man". He must be "machine-made" in the factories of social discipline. In order to survive, the power ruling the masses, which are now satiated with graphs and statistics,[31] galvanizes them and excites them by presenting them with imaginary prospects, a very ambiguous peace, and five-year plans for a terrestrial paradise. However, here in the place of "the new man" is the man of all times who is bored; here and elsewhere, almost everywhere, man is yawning. Dostoievski and Baudelaire said that the world would perish, not by wars but by a gigantic and unbearable boredom when, from a yawn wide as the world, the devil will come forth.

Dostoievski attentively studied this phenomenon which is rapidly becoming universal. He found that the most efficacious method against every evil enterprise is to identify its purest essence, which is immediately shown to be ridiculous; now everything that is manifestly and evidently ridiculous unfailingly kills. Is not the devil himself always somewhat ridiculous?

The writer has drawn largely from the humor of the "fools in Christ", so greatly loved by the people. Protected by their apparent folly, hiding an extreme humility and great fraternal love, during the day they set themselves against guilty silence and denounce without fear every hypocritical profanation with stinging irony and irresistible humor, and during the night they pray for every-

[30] John 4, 14.
[31] The good sense of Disraeli distinguished three degrees of lies: lies, preposterous lies, and statistics.

one. They throw stones at the houses of "the good", and kiss the thresholds of the houses of sinners.

During recent times of bloody persecutions, it was these "poor in spirit" who at the crossroads of cities preached the Gospel and the kingdom of God.

Humor, like laughter, possesses a liberating power; it frees us from the weight of social functions, from every temptation to take ourselves too seriously. It also frees us from excessive suffering in the spiritual life. Frank and childlike gaiety is a typical trait of great saints; they enjoy themselves as children of God, and divine wisdom takes delight in their play.[32]

[32] Prov. 8, 31.

3
Hell and the Infernal
Dimension of the World

Iconography

The icons of the Orthodox Church derive from liturgical texts and from contemplative reading of them. As theology expressed in images, they are related in their function of revelation to the light of Thabor.[33] This feature explains the constant contrast they make between light and darkness, the confrontation of heaven and hell.

Among its charisms, the Johannine Orient, so aware of the resurrection, is also aware of the theme of hell, a theme that St. Paul treats in a compact and striking way in Ephesians 4, 9-10: "Now this, 'he ascended,' what does it mean but that he also first descended into the lower parts of the earth? He who descended, he it is who ascended also above all the heavens, that he might fill all things." We see the astonishing range of the itinerary of the winged lamb between the two extremities, the descent to the lowest point—hell—and the ascension to the highest point—heaven. The Orthodox Church in wonder contemplates "the height and the depth" of the mystery of salvation; it sees in it the dimensions of the charity of Christ and his triumphal message: "Ascending on high, he led away captives" (Eph. 4, 8).

The office of Passion Saturday sings: "You have descended on earth in order to save Adam, O Master, and not finding him there, you have gone even into hell to look for him." The icon of the nativity refers to this text and shows the dense obscurity of a grotto, a black triangle where the child Jesus is lying as in the dark bowels of hell. In order to place himself "in the heart of creation", Christ mystically situates his birth in hell, the point of final despair. Since

[33] The light of Christ transfigured on Mount Thabor.

the time of Adam, men have ended in Sheol, the somber abode of
the dead; it is therefore there that Christ will go seeking them.

In its eschatological aspect, the icon of the nativity, as every
icon, summarizes in a prophetic way all the events of salvation.
By his immobility the Child has already entered into the great
silence of the great sabbath. "Life has gone to sleep and hell shakes
with fear." [34] The swaddling clothes of the infant Jesus have the
exact form of the winding cloths that the angel will show to the
myrrh-bearing women on the morning of the resurrection. The
luminous child stands out in sharp contrast with the black background and anticipates the descent into hell. He is himself "the
light shining in darkness". "The sun has set with him, but the flesh
of God under the earth dissipates the darkness of hell." [35] "Light
battles with darkness; life annihilates death." [36]

From the beginning of his mission, Jesus confronted the cosmic
elements that conceal dark powers—water, air, the desert.[37] An
ideomelon of the epiphany represents the Lord saying to John the
Baptist: "Prophet, come to baptize me . . . I am in a hurry to destroy the enemy hidden in the waters, the prince of darkness, in
order to deliver the world from his nets in granting it eternal life."[38]
In speaking of unsanctified waters, the image of the death-deluge,
the liturgy calls them a "liquid tomb".

In fact, the icon of the epiphany shows Jesus entering into the
waters of the Jordan as if he were entering into a liquid tomb.
This has the form of a cave, containing the entire body of the
Lord (an image of burial reproduced in the sacrament of baptism
by *total immersion*—a figure of the paschal triduum), in order "to
snatch the head of our race from the dark abode".[39] In following
the anticipatory symbolism of the nativity, the icon of the epiphany
shows the pre-descent into hell. "Having descended into the waters,
he bound the strong one."[40]

[34] Office of Holy Saturday.
[35] *Ibid.*
[36] St. Gregory of Nyssa, *P.G.,* 45, 65A.
[37] See O. Rousseau, "La descente aux enfers," *in Mélanges Lebreton.*
[38] Mercenier, *La Prière des Eglises de Rite byzantin,* t. II, p. 292.
[39] St. Cyril of Jerusalem, *P.G.,* 33, 1079.
[40] St. Cyril of Jerusalem, *P.G.,* 33, 441B.

St. Ephrem compares the epiphany to the cross and the ladder "as the ladder that Jacob saw reaching the gate of heaven; on it light descended to baptism . . .";[41] and John of Saroug writes: "Christ on the cross kept himself on earth as on a ladder with many rungs."[42] The cross is "the tree of life planted on Calvary",[43] "the place of the great cosmic struggle".[44] The icon of the crucifixion shows in the vertical branch of the cross, the descent and the ascent of the Word. The *Acts of Andrew* declares: "A part was planted on the earth in order to unite the things on earth and in hell to heavenly things."[45] That is why on the icons, the foot of the cross is sunk into a black cavern where the head of Adam lies, and this is hell.[46] Also on the Orthodox cross, the third transversal board under the feet of the Lord is slightly inclined. The *scabellum pedum*[47] inclined downward represents the destiny of the thief on the left, and the other, inclined upward, represents the destiny of the thief on the right. "Scale of justice"[48] and an opening into eternity, the cross in the middle is like a connecting link between the kingdom and hell.

The icon of the resurrection is that of the "descent into hell".[49] As a liberator, Christ, according to St. Peter, announced to the captives the Gospel of salvation.[50] "You have broken the eternal bars holding the captives."[51] In the silence of Good Friday, the eucharist is not celebrated, for Christ is in hell. For earth it is a day of sorrow, but in hell this Friday is already Easter; death is vanquished and eternal life is proclaimed. The icon shows Christ, the Living One who holds "the keys of death and of hell".[52] He is surrounded by the mandorla, the luminous aureole of glorified

[41] *Hymn*, XI, 11.
[42] *Homily on the Vision of Jacob at Bethel*, n. 95.
[43] Office of the Exaltation of the Holy Cross.
[44] *Pseudo-Hyppolite*, n. 55.
[45] See Daniélou, *Théologie judéo-chrétienne*, p. 312.
[46] Origen, *In Matthew; P.G.*, 1309B.
[47] Acts 2, 35; Ps. 109.
[48] Troparion of None.
[49] The Gospel says nothing about the time of the resurrection.
[50] 1 Pet. 4, 6.
[51] Pentecost Sunday, service of the genuflection.
[52] Apoc. 1, 18.

bodies. His left hand holds a scroll, the proclamation of the resurrection to those who are in hell: "With my right hand I have given
them the baptism of life." [53] "And the Lord extended his hand,
made the sign of the cross on Adam and all the saints, and holding
Adam's right hand, he ascended from hell and all the saints followed him." [54] It is not from the tomb that Christ is coming, but
"from among the dead", coming forth from the former hell as from
a nuptial chamber.

Primitive catechesis drew attention to an aspect of baptism that
has been forgotten in the course of history: baptism *by immersion*
reproduces the figurative curve of salvation, and every baptized
person follows the same itinerary in the footsteps of the Lord. The
sacrament of baptism is then a real descent with Christ in his
death; it is also a *descent into hell*. St. John Chrysostom clearly
says this: "The action of descending into the water and then coming out of it symbolizes the descent into hell and the coming out
from that abode." [55] The light on the Jordan shines in the baptismal
light [56] and signifies the illumination of the infernal darkness.
Enlightened, the baptized person unites sacramentally with the
souls who have mounted with Christ from hell toward eternal life.
Thus baptism is not only dying and rising with Christ, but also
descending into hell and coming out from there, in following him.
This is because hell is more frightful than death. We think of the
words of a Father of the Church: "And the nothingness that they
seek will not be given to them." It is here that the definitive victory has been won.

Christ descended there, laden with the sins of mankind, and he
bore the stigmata of the cross, of crucified Love. We must forcefully emphasize the final and immediate consequences of this.
Every baptized person, risen with Christ, also bears *the stigmata
of the sacerdotal anxieties* of Christ the priest, the stigmata of his
apostolic anguish for the lot of those who are in hell. "There are
places in our heart which do not yet exist, and it is necessary for

---

[53] *Testament en Galilée.*
[54] *Gospel of Nicodemus.*
[55] *Hom. 40,* on 1 Cor. 15, 29. Quoted by O. Rousseau, *op. cit.,* p. 273.
[56] Justin, *P.G.,* 6, 421.

suffering to penetrate there in order that they may come into being," Léon Bloy reminds us. In a vivid image, this care appears in *The Shepherd* of Hermas [57] and in the writings of Clement of Alexandria: [58] the apostles and the doctors descend into hell after death in order to announce salvation and to give baptism to those who ask for it.

Finally the icon of pentecost shows the apostolic college, seated in a luminous circle, receiving the gift of tongues. The contrast is strongly emphasized. Below in an arc and coming out from darkness, is an old king, holding in his hands a linen cloth. On this linen are placed twelve scrolls. Often the arc is separated by a prison grill that stresses the state of captivity. It is the cosmos personified as an old man satiated with the days from the fall, and held a universal captive by the prince of this world. The obscurity that surrounds him signifies "darkness and . . . the shadow of death",[59] the hell from which the non-baptized world stands out; in the brighter portion he aspires to the apostolic light of the Gospel. He holds out his hands to receive grace, and the twelve scrolls symbolize the preaching of the twelve apostles, the universal promise of salvation.

The content of this icon is found in the liturgy of pentecost. The vespers that follow the liturgy of the Sunday contain three great prayers of St. Basil, which the priest reads before the people on their knees, a sign of particular attention. The first prayer presents the Church to the Father; the second asks the Son to safeguard all the living; the third prays for *all* who have died since the creation of the world and thus refers to the descent of Christ into hell. "You who on this final day of pentecost have revealed the mystery of the trinity; you who have sent the vivifying Spirit . . . true knowledge of God . . . you who deign to listen to our prayers of expiation for those who are imprisoned in hell, and who give us the great hope of seeing you, grant them deliverance from their torments . . . give (them) rest in a place of refreshment . . . make

[57] IX, 16, 5-17.
[58] *Strom,* II, 9, 43.
[59] Luke 1, 79.

them worthy of deliverance, for it is not those who are in hell who will have the boldness to confess you; but we the living, we bless you and supplicate you and offer you our prayers and sacrifices for their souls." [60] The superabundant graces of the feast remove all limits. Once a year, on the day of pentecost, the Church prays even for suicides. We see once more the breadth of the feast—from heaven to hell, and from hell to heaven.

[60] Service of the genuflection, Pentecost Sunday. Mercenier, *op. cit.,* p. 389-90.

4
The Suffering
of Men

Without having received a dogmatic definition, the theme of hell and its destiny is constantly present in the liturgy and is universal. Evil is not a substance. A perverted will, conscious and jealous of its autonomy, dynamic in its transgressions of rules, multiplies distances and absences. A wicked being lives as a parasite, forming excrescences and malignant tumors. What he takes from a being, he adds to it in the form of a disease. He can do this, for God has created "another freedom", and the risk that God has taken already proclaims "the man of sorrows" and forecasts the shadow of the cross. According to a saying of the Fathers, God can do all things, except constrain man to love him . . . In the expectation of being loved, God renounces his all-powerfulness and assumes the kenosis [61] under the figure of "the lamb who has been slain from the foundation of the world".[62] His destiny among men depends on the *fiat* of humanity. To assure the liberty of this *fiat,* Christ renounces even his "all-knowledge". The apparent passivity of God hides, according to St. Gregory of Nazianzen, "the suffering of the impassible God". God foresees the worst, and his love does not remain the less vigilant on this account, for man can refuse God and build his life on this refusal. Which one will win, love or freedom? Both are infinite, and hell asks this question.

The East remains foreign to every juridical or penitentiary principle; its conception of sin and its attitude toward the sinner is essentially therapeutic, referring not to a tribunal but to a clinic.

[61] Kenosis: humiliation, abasement, veil of humility hiding the divinity of the Word in his incarnation. Cf. Phil. 2, 7.
[62] Apoc. 13, 8.

Without prejudging anything, the Church abandons herself to God, the lover of men, and redoubles her prayers for the living and the dead. Some, the greatest among the saints, have had the audacity and the charism to pray even for demons. Perhaps the most deadly weapon against the evil one is precisely the prayer of a saint, and perhaps the lot of hell depends also on the charity of the saints. Man himself prepares his own hell in closing himself against divine love that remains unchangeable. "It is not right to say that the sinners in hell are deprived of the love of God . . . But love acts in two different ways, it becomes suffering in the damned and joy in the blessed." [63]

Every faithful member of the Orthodox Church, in approaching the holy table, confesses: "I am the first of sinners", which means the greatest, or more exactly, without any possible measure or comparison, "the unique sinner". St. Ambrose, as a pastor and a liturgist, explains it and gives it a concise and striking form: "The same man is at the same time condemned and saved." [64] St. Isaac, as an ascetic, gives another: "The one who sees his sin is greater than the one who raises the dead to life." Such a vision of reality leads to a final and paradoxical conclusion. A very simple man confessed to St. Anthony: "In watching the passersby, I say to myself, 'All will be saved, I alone shall be damned.' " St. Anthony concluded: "Hell really exists, but for me alone." This love of men is answered by the magnificent words of a Mohammedan mystic: "If you place me among those in Gehenna, I shall pass my eternity in speaking to them of my love for you." [65]

In repeating St. Ambrose's words, we can say that the world in its totality is "at the same time condemned and saved". Even more, perhaps hell in its very condemnation finds its own transcendence. It seems that this is the meaning of the words Christ

[63] St. Isaac the Syrian, *P.G.*, 34, 5440. Cf. Origen, *De Prin.*, III, 6, 5; St. Gregory of Nyssa, *Catech. Discourse*, XXVI, 5, 9: *Comment. on Ephes.*, III, 10 of Ambrosiaster.

[64] *P.L.*, 15, col. 1502, quoted by O. Clement, *Notes sur le Mal*, in *Contacts*, no. 31, p. 204.

[65] René Khawam, *Propos d'amour des mystiques musulmans* (Paris, 1960).

is supposed to have said to Sylvain of Athos, a contemporary staret: "Keep your spirit in hell but do not despair." [66]

Péguy reproached Dante for having visited hell "as a tourist". The great spiritual leaders have another way of descending there.[67] "The light of Christ enlightens every man coming into the world," says the prayer of Prime; even unconsciously, all bear its mysterious signs. It is not for Christians to despair then, but to hear Christ saying to the Church one of the gravest sentences that it is given her to hear for her apostolate: "He who receives you, receives me . . ." The fate of the world depends on our art of being witnesses to pentecost; it depends also on our inventive charity in the face of the dimension of evil of the world.

All that theology teaches on the condemnation of the world is in the phrase: "Cain, where is your brother Abel?" In addition, there is the mystery of the Church in the light of the priestly prayer of Christ (John 17), in "Abel, where is your brother Cain?" The love of God was "in the beginning" (1 John 4, 9-10) as an event transcending every response to it. The two paracletes come to save. Love, in its profoundest depths, appears disinterested, like the pure joy of the friend of the bridegroom, like the joy that subsists by itself, a joy *a priori* to everything.

In John 14, 28, Jesus asks us to rejoice with a great joy, the reason of which is beyond man, namely, the objective existence of God. In this radiant and royally free joy lies the salvation of the world. John 13, 20 invites us to discover the manner in which we can be accepted, "received" by the world. It is now the hour for the Church no longer to speak of Christ, but *to become Christ*. The heavenly mansion extends its walls even to the confines of the world, even though it is here a question of the world in revolt, in opposition to God. *God loved the world even when it was in sin.*[68] The bride takes on the face of her spouse in the eucharistic bread, communion, friendship. Her light shines not merely to shine but to change the night into a day that never ends.

[66] Quoted by Arch. Sophrony, *Messager de l'Ex. du Patr. Russe,* no. 26, p. 96.
[67] See Arch. Spiridon, *Mes missions en Sibérie* (Paris, 1950), p. 44.
[68] John 3, 16; 12, 32.

More than ever before, the world seeks for something that would unite men; it seeks for "the human brother". It is here that Christian charity alone—the kind that does not calculate or measure or limit—can cause the light of the Christian world to shine in the direction of the one farthest from Christ, for it is in this one that Christ is waiting to be received. St. Symeon called himself "the poor brother of all men", and he really was this. The new man is not being fabricated in the Marxist factories of social discipline. The "new creature" has his origin in the Holy Spirit, who forms apostolic souls; he takes his faith seriously and does things that are very simple when seen in the light of evangelical faith—raising the dead when the Lord tells him to do so. This critical hour is so fearful that it calls upon all the powers of faith, and that is why St. Peter quotes the prophecy of Joel and announces an abundance of gifts, with pentecost redoubling its outpourings in pre-apocalyptic times.

Every baptized person is invisibly *stigmatized* since he bears within him the deep wound of the destiny of others, of all others; he adds something to the suffering of Christ who is in agony until the end of the world. "To imitate" Christ is to follow him in his descent to the bottom of the gulf of our world. "Imitation" is configuration to the total Christ; it is martyrdom, according to Origen,[69] for "The love of God and the love of men are two aspects of a single total love".[70] My personal attitude, which is always unique, is to fight against *my hell,* which threatens me if I do not love enough to save others. Still, an almost imperceptible inclination toward activism leads me to say: "I love you in order to save you." An apostolic soul says: "I save you because I love you . . ." During each liturgical service we sing: "We have seen the true light, we have received the heavenly Spirit." Every Sunday is a renewal of pentecost. This versicle expresses the truth, but in giving its gift, it makes an urgent appeal to spread this overwhelming experience of light into the hell of today's world.

---

[69] *Exhortatio ad martirium.*
[70] St. Maximus, *P.G.,* 91, 409B.

5
Message of Pentecost

"The kingdom of God is within you." The beating of the heart of the Gospel can be heard in these words. The two worlds draw near each other, the frontiers are blurred, the beyond becomes the here and now. Every believer, taking part in the liturgy, has this experience: "Now all the heavenly powers invisibly co-celebrate with us." However, these eruptions of "the wholly other" mean that hell is also in the midst of us. In spite of the clearness of this idea,[71] the same term is applied to many situations in life. We hear of the hell of an unhappy love affair, the hell of conjugal life, the hell of the presence of others, the hell of oneself. Hell in the guise of man forces its way into our intimacy, becomes a familiar element, well-known but terrifying. Certainly it is different from the image presented by the masters of the Middle Ages, of Bosch, Goya, or the *danse macabre;* it is nevertheless real. The devil sets aside his romantic mask and becomes as familiar as Ivan Karamazov's devil dressed in a business suit, or as anybody else, and as such we perhaps meet him every day. He is no longer disguised as an archangel with burnt wings. Truer, more human, and for that reason more to be feared, he resembles us. Marcel Jouhandeau has expressed the essential things: "By myself, I can set up in the face of God an empire over which he can do nothing; this is hell . . . man does not understand hell because he does not understand his own heart." [72]

The titanic power of refusing God is the most advanced position of human freedom; liberty has been willed thus by God, that is, without limits. "God cannot force anyone to love him," as the Fathers teach. This, one scarcely dares to say it, is the hell of his

[71] See von Balthasar, *Dieu et l'homme d'aujourd'hui* (Paris, 1958).
[72] Quoted by von Balthasar, *op. cit.,* p. 245.

love, the heavenly dimension of hell, the desolate vision of man repeating to satiety the action of Adam or of Judas, fleeing into the darkness of solitude. Not all the wrong is on their side; they have acted thus because of their ignorance of the graces of pentecost and because of the lamentable absence of true witnesses. An acid pessimism eats into the roots of their lives, making them indifferent and impermeable to grace. It is from the hell of their hearts that they hurl toward an empty heaven their despair and their blasphemies. The satanic paradise of the proletarian empire produces the poison of an enormous boredom. This empire, strong in all techniques, causes the abandonment of man to himself, an abandonment equal in vastness to the interplanetary spaces where rockets take the place of angels and where the thunder of God's wrath is beginning to rumble.

It is no longer possible to reduce faith or atheism to a "private affair". Our time is indeed the age of universalism—the catholicity of the kingdom or of the anti-kingdom. The world beyond, whether sacred or secularized, is posited in the apocalyptic dimensions of our existence. It excludes any "between the two", and implacably obliges us to choose between two totalitarianisms— "God is all in all", or "God is not anywhere". The intermediate type, that of Max Stirner, for example, that Kleinbürgerlich, that petty bourgeois Prometheus, who stole fire from heaven to heat his coffee and to light his pipe, is disappearing from the world scene. For the religious needs of the human spirit, the dominant new philosophies offer their own absolutes, their stimulants and their mystic intoxications. "Certainly," wrote Simone Weil, "there is an intoxication in being a member of the mystical body of Christ. But today many mystical bodies, which do not have Christ as their head, procure for their members intoxications that are, in my opinion, of the same nature." [73]

Present-day science is no longer a dream. As a dream, it has been realized magnificently and beyond all expectations. Its rapid progression is becoming unforeseeable; it is going beyond the laboratories of scientists, and it is indispensable in any meditation on being, the existence of man and his destiny. It is not theology

[73] *L'Attente de Dieu,* p. 87.

nor philosophy that is changing the face of the world; it is science. Cybernetics and automation are providing the human brain with a marvelous complement; they permit very exact forecasts which concern all men. Power over biological processes and over the spaces around the earth places in human consciousness a new spirit of prophecy. By the solidarity that in fact exists, all men find that they have a common destiny that entails its own risks. Scientists cry out to us in their anxiety. "I am a man," said Harold Urcy, "who is afraid and who wishes to share his fear." [74] This is because science and techniques intervene in a *political context,* bringing to it a power over men that is almost unlimited, as is shown in George Orwell's *1984.*

Humanity is exposed to the risk of being reduced to rationally conditioned gestures, foreseen in advance, with its critical faculties controlled or inhibited. A balanced interaction between material progress and spiritual growth is seen to be more and more problematic, and the future that is opening up is in part darkened by shadows. An existence that has broken with God is built on this refusal of God. Science, good in itself, risks finding itself set up entirely against God. The Antichrist of the *Legend* by V. Soloviev presents himself as a great benefactor of humanity, as an accomplished scientist, offering as bread the miracles of techniques and peace.

The situation of the modern world calls upon the Christian conscience, questions it, accuses it. If Communism exists, it is because Christians, unfaithful to the Gospel, have not been able to bring about the kingdom of God on earth. If present-day thought has such an accent of despair and emptiness, it is because Christian hope has lost "the consolation afforded by the Scriptures",[75] and is no longer on the plane of the divine promise. If abstract art exists, it is because figurative art no longer represents anything, for it incarnates no spirit and radiates no light; surrealism arises only where men have lost the flame of things and the secret contents of the real. The prodigies of technology, according to Apocalypse 13, 13, only parody the fires of pentecost. In the heart of an infernal

[74] *Sommes-nous en révolutions* (1958), p. 45.
[75] Rom. 15, 4.

existence, man feels himself abandoned to his total solitude. Sheol signifies a place of darkness, and hell in Greek, the place where one does not see, where no glance meets that of another; hell knows no vis-à-vis, no meeting face to face. It is a place where there are "the tears of the victims with none to comfort them".[76]

Here the message of pentecost is seen in all its breadth. Speaking for all men, Christ has uttered the cry: "Why hast thou abandoned me?" This cry has shaken the foundations of hell and moved the heart of the Father, but the Father who sent his Son knows that even hell is his domain and that "the door of death" is changed into "a door of life". Even infernal despair is touched by a hope that it formerly contained, and it is not for Christians to despair. The hand extended toward Christ never remains empty. The fourth Gospel shows us Judas holding out his hand. In placing there the eucharistic bread,[77] Christ made his last appeal to evil, to night at its darkest. Judas' fingers closed over the immolated lamb. Judas went out and "it was night". St. Augustine has this word to say: "He who went out was himself night." [78] The night received him and hid his terrible communion with Satan. Satan is in Judas. Judas carries away in his hand, which is that of Satan, a fearful mystery. Hell keeps in its breast that morsel of bread. Is not this particle of light the faithful and exact expression of the words, "the light shines in darkness"? The gesture of Jesus designated the last mystery of the Church: she is the hand of Jesus offering the eucharistic bread, addressing her appeal to all, for all are in the power of the prince of this world. The light does not yet dissipate the darkness, but the darkness has no ascendancy over the invincible light.[79] We are all in the final tension of divine love.

On this level we find not the denial but the exigency of hell, which comes from human freedom. Confronted with God, who

[76] Eccles. 4, 1.

[77] This is the opinion of St. Ephrem, St. John Chrysostom, St. Ambrose, St. Augustine, St. Jerome.

[78] See Lelong, *Saint Jean parmi nous* (Paris, 1961), p. 138.

[79] John 1, 5. The Vulgate translates "the darkness did not receive him" — *non comprehenderunt*. The East follows Origen and translates: "the darkness did not conquer him." Both are true: the resistance of the darkness and the invincibility of the light.

forces no one, hell testifies to our freedom of loving God. This engenders hell, for man can always say: "May thy will not be done", and even God has no control over this decision.

God is a *mysterium fascinosum,* absolutely and for all eternity. He is not a clever architect with perfectly balanced plans. There is the cross planted at the threshold of a new life. A folly and a scandal, it upsets every design that is too geometrical, or "Euclidian", as Dostoievski would say. Through the reasoning of our heart, we feel that our image of God would become disturbing if God does not love his creature even to punishing him; it would also be disturbing if God does not save the loved one without touching or destroying his freedom.

"Hell is other people," Sartre declares. A Christian can say: "The destiny of others is my hell." The Father has given all judgment to the Son of Man, and it is "the judgment of the judgment",[80] the judgment crucified. "The Father is crucifying love, the Son is crucified love, the Holy Spirit is the invincible love of the cross." [81] This invincible power shines forth in the effusion of the Holy Spirit and every baptized person receives it. If the despairing explore the depths of Satan, the Gospel calls upon believers "to move mountains". Perhaps this means for us to move the infernal mountain of the modern world and its nothingness toward the dazzling light of pentecost and its new life: "I have today set before you life . . . and death." The "night" of the Western mystics, and "the abandonment by God" of the Eastern spiritual leaders, speak of the descent into hell. For the one who is attentive to the world, the experience of hell is immediate.

In the Orthodox services of Matins on the night of Easter, in the silence of the end of Saturday, the priest and people leave the church. The procession stops at the exterior, before the closed door of the church. For a brief moment, this door symbolizes the Lord's tomb, death, hell. The priest makes the sign of the cross on the door, and under its irresistible force, the door opens wide and all enter the church, which is flooded with light, singing: "Christ has

[80] St. Maximus, *P.G.,* 90, 408D.
[81] Metr. Philaretes of Moscow, *Oraisons, homélies et discours,* translated into French by A. Sturdza (Paris, 1849), p. 154.

risen from the dead, he has vanquished death by death, and he has given life to *all* those who are in the tombs." *The gate of hell has become again the door of the church.* One can go no further in the symbolism of the feast. Yes, the world in its totality is at the same time condemned and saved; it is at the same time hell and the kingdom of God.

When we confess in the Apostles' Creed that "I believe in the Holy Spirit, in the Holy Catholic Church", we mean "in the Holy Spirit that descended on the Church on pentecost", and this is pentecost perpetuated and the parousia begun in action in history. This time does not withdraw man from the world but it lightens the weight of the world, making man more joyous by the breath of the Spirit. It is in our world of television, guided space craft, super-sonics, interplanetary journeys, in this world that is at the same time atheistic and believing, paradisiacal and infernal, but always loved by God, that man is called upon to live the miracle of his faith. Like Abraham in former times, he starts out without knowing where he is going or why; but he knows that he bears in his heart a flame of fire, and he can only repeat the winged words of St. John Climacus: "I go forward singing to you . . ."

6
The Fathers of
the Desert

In the struggle without respite against evil, the evil one, and hell, the remarkable effort of the Fathers of the desert and later of monasticism has played a decisive role in the destiny of Christianity. Following them, today's believer takes up the same task that has been enormously lightened, and lives on the heritage of this glorious and highly instructive past.

The eschatological texts of Scripture place history between the incarnation and the parousia. Time appears entirely relative to the return of Christ who will surprise us "as a thief in the night". Qualitatively, since the day of pentecost, we live in the latter days, and the parousia that has begun despoils the centuries of their apparent stability. For "those who love his coming",[82] the Christian city that the Empire of Constantine undertook to build is profoundly ambiguous, and this is why the monastic ascesis of virginity would like to hasten the end of the world by the extinction of the human species. If a couple began history, it is abstinence that will end it, Dositheus affirmed in the 3rd century. A little later, Basil of Ancyra wrote: "Now that the earth has been inseminated . . . virginity . . . will cause incorruption to flourish, beginning with the body." [83] The vow of celibacy, the *collective* refusal of procreation, expresses an extreme position in regard to history and the future of life on earth. The Gospel image of a sudden death accentuates the moribund state of the world, which bearing its own agony, advances from one survival to another, toward its inevitable disappearance. Consequently the radical break of monasticism with society was required.

[82] 2 Tim. 4, 8. Apparition here has the meaning of the second coming of Christ.
[83] *Sur la virginité*, p. 55.

A very paradoxical reversal of the situation appears here. It is no longer the pagan world that fights and eliminates the martyr; it is the hermit who takes up the attack and eliminates the world from his being. The Fathers brought back the atmosphere of fighting of the first centuries, finding the equivalent of the aggressive forms of persecution. The arenas where wild beasts had torn the martyrs apart were replaced by the immense desert where more fearful beasts rise up, and where the demoniacal powers cast their shadows. The "temptation of St. Anthony" or that of John of Egypt offers the striking image of temptation by the evil one so faithfully reproduced in the art of Jerome Bosch.

In burying themselves in vast solitudes, the anchorites sought to penetrate the territory of the demons in order to fight them more efficaciously at close range. They made a desert for themselves, a desert of themselves, more agonizing than merely an uninhabited place, a simple retreat. It was this solitude willed by the human spirit that was visited by the noonday devil and the one of nocturnal despair. Only an ascetic charged with extreme vigor could take the exact measure of the adversary and confront him "in a very singular combat", according to the words of St. Benedict.

The rupture with the world went further than a mere flight from the approach of man. Those seeking unusual perfection placed themselves at the edge of the world, not to find a refuge, but to build a new world, and to anticipate the heavenly city. The ascetics considered desert places as an intermediary zone between the profane world and the kingdom. Exile became the pilgrimage of *homo viator* seeking his heavenly origins. The hermits were not exiles but "athletes of exile", fighters at the most advanced outposts; above all, they were, in the magnificent words of St. Macarius, "men intoxicated with God".[84] When in groups, they foreshadowed the future societies or republics of monks (Mount Athos) which were built not on the edge but on the site of this world, and which by their very nature are the radical negations of profane society. For the one who turns completely toward the Orient, conformity is unacceptable.

According to the firm belief of his disciples, St. Pachomius estab-

[84] *Homélies,* 18, 7.

lished his monastic community, which counted eight thousand members, on "the rule of the angel" who dictated it to him. The two letters that he left to his successors are written in an unknown language, called "the language of the angels". This symbolism is indicative of the transcendent origin of monastic society which contrasts sharply with bases of the city of man. An anchorite is God's rebel, and "the monastery is an earthly heaven", St. John of Climacus declares.[85] He proclaims the abolition of profane history and announces the coming of the new city inhabited by new men. If every man is made "similar" to the image of God, the office of the holy monks calls them "very similar", and venerates them as "earthly angels and heavenly men".

Leaving a world entails entering another and implies a consistent strategy. A preliminary ascesis *undoes* the tainted heritage in order to *remake* a purified human being. It experiments on the "anti-natural", anti-conformity conditions of life, as if the world of the living no longer existed or as if it presented only a deceptive and unreal aspect of being. In order to apply the axe of repentance to the roots of guilty conformity and behavior, the "dying to the world" practiced in the extreme forms of the ascesis of the desert strikes us by its deliberate asymmetry, which at times reaches an apparent ugliness, the exact opposite of the profane ideal of ethics and aesthetics.

Thus "the grazers", descending to the level of the soil, nourished themselves on herbs and roots. They took the attitude of Adam hiding in the bushes; they fled from men and made themselves akin to the animal world. St. Ephrem the Syrian, called "the zither of the Holy Spirit", wrote in his *Praise of the Solitaries:* "They went wandering in the deserts with the wild beasts as if they themselves were wild beasts." They lived as if they had cast off the burden of the flesh, and in their emaciation they retained no accumulated poisons. In appearance they imitated animal life, putting on a second nature just as those accomplished actors, "the fools of Christ", in order to create an atmosphere of contempt and abjection, and to become "the least" of this world in reaching the utmost limit of humility.

[85] *The Heavenly Ladder,* 27th degree.

"The recluses" also led a strange life; giving up light and language, they buried themselves in ancient tombs or in holes in the ground. We can see in this form the trials of abandonment, solitude and silence, this experience anticipating the conditions of death. "Pray often in the tombs and paint an indelible picture of them in your heart," [86] St. John Climacus counseled everyone, in order to make death familiar, to live and meditate on its mystery before it comes. The recluses opposed the silence of the lips to the tumult of a soul on fire with passion. "Do not judge anyone and learn to be silent," said St. Macarius, for in the words of St. Isaac: "Silence will be the language of the future world." [87]

There were also "the dendrites" chained to a branch of a tree so that they would no longer touch the earth sullied by man. Like Noah in the ark, they relived the experience of humanity withdrawn by the grace of God from a contaminated world. By this withdrawal they measured the depth of man's fall and their penitent tears mingled the waters of the deluge with the waters of baptism. In tree branches, exposed to the winds, they led the life of birds intoxicated with the heavens and with God.

"The stationaries" remained motionless and petrified, with their arms in the form of a cross in a state of perpetual prayer, a living symbol of the vertical vocation of man, of his spirit that tends to the most high. "The stylites" continued this attitude. Perched on high columns, far above all agitation or tumult, they placed themselves between heaven and earth, though nearer heaven on the last rung of the "Ladder of Paradise".

All these forms of withdrawal represent a very puzzling phenomenon. The ascetics' refusal of the human city and of historical development brought about a return to the conditions of *prehistoric* life. The words, "become as little children", were taken literally, but this "spiritual childhood" hides an astonishing depth. We read in St. Isaac's works: "When you prostrate yourself before God in prayer, become in your own judgment like an ant, a worm,

[86] *Ibid.,* 18th degree.
[87] A. J. Wensinck, *Mystic Treatises of Isaac of Nineveh,* p. 115.

or a beetle. Do not speak before God as a man who knows anything, but stammer and approach him with a childlike spirit." [88]

Exteriorly this ascesis strikes us as an extravagance bordering on the inhuman, but interiorly we discover a great sobriety and perfect moderation. Some of the words of the ascetics, such as those of Hesychius on the silence of the heart, a state of perfect recollection, reveal a profound knowledge of the human soul.

The extraordinary and the miraculous do not surprise us in the atmosphere of the desert. They become normal for a nature that is inwardly on fire. Thus "the old man Joseph arose and lifted his hands toward heaven. His hands became as lighted candles. And he said to Abbot Lot: 'If you wish to be perfect, become all on fire.'" [89] The ascesis of the desert entailed the baptism of fire.

It is a great temptation for an historian to regard this ascesis as an aberration and to give "a comical description" [90] of it. A university professor of the 20th century would automatically reduce its secret depths to its surface appearance, and he would do this less by what he says than by what he does not say and by what he does not even suspect. When the desert Fathers recognized the

[88] Wensinck, *op. cit.*, p. 343.

[89] *Apopht. patrum*, Joseph, 6.

[90] The expression is that of Father Rousselot in regard to the book by J. Lacarriere, *Men Intoxicated with God*. The author of this book presents a valuable collection of facts and texts, but he remains on the exterior and does not touch upon any of the contemporary commentaries on this dramatic chapter of Christian spirituality. He in no way commits himself, remaining strictly objective, but such an attitude is ambiguous and implies a tacit judgment. In this perspective, it is instructive to study, following Aldous Huxley, the bio-chemical effects due to starvation, to exercises of the type "I kill my body because it is killing me," to high temperature, and to darkness, or to compare Christian hesychasts to Indian yogi who make experiments with respiration; in diminishing it, they lessen the wear on the heart. All these phenomena are met with in the Himalayas as in the Thebaid, and spring from the same techniques, but they are insufficient as explanations. The bio-chemical processes are natural reactions of the organism; used ascetically, they can at most facilitate the manifestations of the spirit. But every technical means that is used only leads to and stops at the threshold of the transcendent, as for example, the "prayer of Jesus". The critical mind can describe the threshold, but it can go no further, for beyond there it does not apply and does not explain anything.

powerlessness of words, they counseled veneration of the mystery
by silence. This is just what the icon does. An icon of a saint tells
us nothing of his physical appearance and gives no biographical,
historical, or sociological detail. It shows the radiating influence of
the man beyond history. A saint bears history within himself, but
he shows it in a different manner; he reveals a new dimension of
it, in which its meaning is made clear by its last end. He constitutes a meta-historical synthesis. We must read the lives of the
desert Fathers *iconographically,* just as we contemplate an icon.

To pose the alternative of culture *or* holiness [91] is like breaking
down an open door. A well-balanced tradition would affirm culture *and* holiness. However, to make this balance and to establish
it definitely, it was necessary first to pass dialectically through the
extreme polarization of the terms. In effecting this passage, the
ascesis of the desert reveals its Gospel origin. The Holy Spirit led
Jesus into the desert to encounter the devil. The mysterious time of
forty days of silence inaugurated the mission of the Word. "He who
truly possesses the Word of Jesus can hear even his silence," declared St. Ignatius of Antioch.[92] The tradition of the Church is
precisely this prayerful silence which surrounds the Word and
from which the liturgy and the icon come forth. Silence and the
Word, holiness and culture, compenetrate and complement one
another.

It would be a flagrant error to see in the desert only the outcasts
of monasticism, illiterate men living in a degrading atmosphere. If
we do not penetrate into the deep motives of their souls, we pass
by a unique fact that had incalculable consequences for the destiny
of Christianity. The ascesis of the desert forms an inevitable moment in Christian spirituality. Certainly it belongs to a past age,
and any return to the desert *now* would be an unacceptable rupture
with tradition. Nevertheless, this ascesis keeps its *unfailing significance for all ages and all times;* it is the keystone of later
monastic tradition.

It was not with the instruments of culture but with their bare

[91] Taken from the work of Father Festugière, that is excellent in other
respects.
[92] Eph. 15, 2.

hands that the ascetics maintained the Christian ideal at its transcendent height, and this is the miracle. They understood well the spirit of the Gospel; it is not the road that is impossible, it is the impossible that is the road, and they have traversed it.

Above all, every ascesis exercises a pedagogical influence. A man of the world, even the one most laden with cares, knew that somewhere, *in his place,* there were true men, who in the silence of their hearts were speaking with angels and who were encroaching on the life of the future world. Crowds used to come to contemplate the stylites, and they had engraved on their hearts this image of "intoxication with God". Some of them, in order to have it always before their eyes, made a summary sketch of it and thus traced the prototype of the icon.

"By the virtue of the Spirit and spiritual regeneration, man is raised to the dignity of the first Adam,"[93] said St. Macarius. The ascesis lessens the effects of the first sin and manifests the power of the spirit. The "bestiaries" of the desert recount an astonishing friendship, for the wild beasts recognized "the odor of paradise" in the saints and ended by becoming more human, reflecting the human face with its gentle and intelligent eyes. The anchorites revived man's lost privilege, given to him by God, to rule the animals and to be king of the universe.[94]

The world finds its norm, its scale of comparison, in the extreme efforts of the ascetics; it perceives also the dreadful dullness and insipidity of the spirit of self-sufficiency. In the face of the declaration of common sense, "God does not ask so much of us", the ascesis of the desert proclaims the terrible jealousy of God, who after giving all of himself, asks all from men. The desert Fathers have left us a picture of this total gift. Its excessive features strike our attention and ask us what is the utmost each one of us can do. The Christian type would not be what it is were it not for this ascesis, which from remote times has unconsciously made its purifying influence felt.

We can go deeper still. The ascetics renounced culture in their

---

[93] *Homélies spirituelles.*
[94] They are a living commentary on Mark 1, 13.

seeking for the one thing necessary. This desire had to become a
passion for perfection: "Sell all that you *have*." Even more, "Sell
all that you *are*." In the perfection of this attitude, all became a
single act—the carrying of the cross. "Let him renounce himself
and take up his cross." This is not the liturgy, but is a preliminary
to it, a compact and startling epitome of immolation.

"Ground between the two millstones of humility", the ascetics
sacrificed themselves in order that others would later profit from
their "virginity of spirit", by inaugurating Christian culture. The
ascesis in itself is not the ideal; it represents only the culminating
point of the catharsis or purification. Tertullian, as an already
prejudiced polemist, asked: [95] "What does Athens have in common
with Jerusalem, and the Academy with the Church?" He added:
"All curiosity *ceases* after the Gospel." Now all curiosity really
begins after the Gospel, but in a different manner than before.

There is a risk that peace will allow this curiosity to slacken.
The ascesis of the desert, after having interiorized the persecutions,
will later interiorize true peace in hesychasm, but this time with
the contemplative knowledge of God and of the world in the light
of Thabor.

The ascesis *undoes* the act by which Adam ceased to be fully
himself, in wishing to belong only to himself and in refusing to go
beyond himself in God. It takes up again the vocation of Adam and
continues the conformation to Christ *obeying*. The martyrs imitated
Christ crucified; the ascetics "imitated", took literally the counsels
of the Gospel: "If thy hand . . . thy foot . . . are an occasion of
sin for thee, cut them off. If thy eye is an occasion of sin to thee,
pluck it out . . . it is better for thee to enter the kingdom of God
lame and with one eye than to be cast into the hell of fire . . . for
everyone shall be salted with fire." In the heroic atmosphere of
the desert this salt and this fire were not simple metaphors. The
moral chaining of the instincts by the will was realized here by
means of actual and heavy chains. Their spiritual elevation caused
the stylites to mount pillars. St. Anthony attained at the same time
the summit of meditation and the peak of Kolzum. The arid and
burning desert flourished as "a spiritual meadow". Through the

[95] *De praescr. haer.*, 7.

ascetics' thirst for the kingdom, monasteries and deserts were transformed into microcosmic particles of the heavenly city of the future.

The soul that has been drawn from nothingness desires to find its origins and asks to be recreated, to allow itself to be unmade and remade by having its elements purified one after another. The goal aimed at by the ascetics was a state anterior to fallen nature in its preconceptual, preaffective, prevoluntary center; they sought to reach the unsullied structure of the "self" made to the image of God. In the extreme forms of ascesis, we perceive the attempt to change the human condition by the mutation of its psychosomatic elements. St. Macarius says this in his *Homilies:* "When the apostle urges the putting off of the old man, he means the entire man. He means: have other eyes than those the man has, another head than his, hands and feet that are no longer his." St. Symeon the New Theologian speaks as a mystic in his *Hymns:* "My hands are those of an unfortunate and my feet are those of Christ. I, unworthy, am the hand and the foot of Christ. I move my hand and my hand is all Christ, for the divinity of God is invisibly united to me."

"The apostolic man" of the spiritual writers is not subject to the laws of this world; he anticipates the man of eternity. The radical character of the change is emphasized by the fact that, though it is interior, it modifies, in certain cases, even outward appearance. This was the case of St. Alexis, the "man of God", who after his life in the desert was received as a beggar in his own home without being recognized. A woman named Athanasia joined her husband in the desert with the features of a man and was not recognized until the moment of her death. All ties, as well as sexual differentiation, became foreign to them and they to the world.

The ascetic technique "renders the earthly qualities of the body pure". An athlete exercises his body; an ascetic, his flesh. The icons show us men whose flesh has neither weight nor earthly heaviness, beings living in a new dimension. They have lost their material qualities that made them like things, but not their reality; more real than anyone else, they have gone beyond themselves.

The ascesis of solitude dims even the light and colors of the outer world in order to direct the glance inward. The ascetics manifested a supreme indifference to social conventions. "Clothed with space", they often went naked, having found again a lost innocence. They did not wish to harm even the smallest insect, and they acted not from without and *on,* but from within with a boundless cosmic charity.

Their refusal of a contaminated world led to the abolition of all social traditions. The extreme forms of their ascesis effected a deliberate regression to the prenatal, mineral, animal stage, and a behavior that was opposed to the normal human condition. It led to an Adam-like nakedness, to a physical and psychic indifference, in despoiling men of their human attributes—upright posture, discursive reasoning, speech, rest. The ascetics ceased reacting *normally* to the needs of the flesh in order to purify at the roots all the essential elements of a human being, and to reconstitute a new man, spiritually and also biologically. The Orient conceives salvation from a therapeutic point of view; it sees in it, before all else, a cure of death by eternal life. It avoids juridical wording, and expresses redemption itself in biological terms: it is not so much the fault that is repaired as the nature that is repaired in Christ.

Ascesis means that the encounter with God cannot be effected by starting from fallen nature. God remains exterior in the proportion that the passions are interior and the "ego" is identified with "the dark spirits that nestle somewhere near the heart".[96] The ascent toward God begins with a descent into oneself—"Know thyself" —in order to force the *deifugal* passions to alienate and exteriorize themselves. This first stage is called *praxis,* the practice of purifying and exteriorizing virtues. To be despised and struck by all serves as a purging against concupiscence, explained St. John Climacus [97] in speaking of humility. Though the avoidance of all speculative thought may give the impression of "stultification", it is only a preliminary method in the search of "the place of the heart", of "the place of God". However, every seeking of the natural "buries the heart under the fog of passions", arouses an immediate reaction

[96] Diadochus of Photike, *Chapitres sur la perfection spirituelle,* 33.
[97] *P.G.,* 88, 717A-B.

from the dark "underground", from the obscure world of the sub-conscious.

With great psychotherapeutic shrewdness, these spiritual men discovered the obscure energies lying below the threshold of consciousness.

The ascesis of the desert is a vast psychoanalysis followed by a psychosynthesis of the universal human soul. Origen, the brilliant commentator, compares the desert to Plato's cave. The desert with all its arsenal of phantasmagoria was a *theater of shadows,* a spectacle for men and angels; only the shadows did not reflect the reality outside the cave. They were the projection of the world inside man.

For the authors of the New Testament, as for the Fathers of the desert, the world before the time of Christ was a world bewitched. The Gospel speaks of the possessed, of disturbing elements and of the perversity of the human heart. The abysses we discover are *haunted;* there are secret places where evil powers are crouching and they rule us if we are ignorant or heedless. Ascesis cultivates our attention and begins by an experimental phenomenology of our human interior. It was necessary to materialize and personalize the perverted elements of a being, the hateful ego with its self-love, the doubter and the demoniacal counterpart. Above all, it was necessary to extirpate them, to "vomit" them, and to objectify them, in order to look them in the face as detached and exteriorized. This "objectivation" creates a distance, permits the projection of all interior elements as on a screen (Plato's cave of shadows) under the form of monsters, wild beasts and demons. This operation requires a very precise conviction of the reality of the enemy, in order to cut every bond and communion with him. Jerome Bosch gives an artistic interpretation in his striking iconography.

The Fathers of the desert have carried out this operation once for all and in the place of all. "He who has seen himself such as he is and has seen his sin is greater than he who raises the dead." [98] They have shown man naked, and they have put a face and name on every obscure element of evil. The hidden play, both human

[98] St. Isaac the Syrian, *Sentences,* 50.

and demoniacal, is demonstrated and brought to light. After this demonstration, the man going to confession knows what he has to do and what is going to happen. Each time he reproduces the experience of the desert Fathers. He can look within himself, but *now* without being troubled by the unknown. In order not to remain in a stifling tête-à-tête with his sins and with himself, he can discern their elements and exteriorize them by confession. Here only Christ, the absolute innocent and the absolute victim, can bring about the unique living transference, "by cancelling the decree against us".[99]

When the ascesis left the caves of the desert and spread through the world, the screen and the shadows disappeared. All entered again into the interior of man but in a *different* manner. The hierarchy of purified values, having been reestablished, permitted man to see the evil before being tempted to commit it.

The metaphysical unity of mankind, the collective subconsciousness lying at the roots of consciousness, condition and explain the mystical fact that humanity was different before the incarnation from what it is now. One can say also that human consciousness was different before the ascesis of the desert from what it was after. Just like the event of pentecost, this ascesis has modified the dominant energies of the psyche and has renewed the human spirit.

The therapeutic effect formed by "the desert" in the profoundest depths of the human spirit is universal. It represents the collective vomit, the objectivation and the projection on the outside of the original and the accumulated impurity. This is perhaps the meaning of the words of St. Paul, "to add to the suffering of Christ", something that the innocent Christ could not do in the place of man; only the sinner, the man of the desert, could do it in the place of all and with a universal significance. From a positive point of view, it was *the formation of the ascetic archetype of man*. It pre-formed "the violent" in order to fight evil and the evil one inside and outside of man.

Human guilt does not do away with the reality of demons. That authorities of the stature of St. Athanasius, St. Cassian and St. Benedict speak of demons should give greater prudence to every

[99] Col. 2, 14.

critical spirit who sees in them only obscurantism. The reality is more complex. The Gospel speaks of them, and the rite of exorcism bears testimony to them.

The Gospel [100] speaks of the unclean spirit who, finding a human soul "swept and decorated", installs himself there again with seven other spirits. The ascesis has purified the soul; it also keeps its role of vigilant sentinel.

Certainly *now* there can be no possible return to the desert. We are in different times and above all in different *spiritual ages.* Delays on one side and advances on the other do not allow exact dating, but it is clear that on the margin of chronology men, for example, Evagrius, the Macarius of the *Homilies,* and Diadochus, belong to another age than did the ascetics of the desert. The collective projection is over, and every attempt to revive it would become a dangerous illusion. Excessive analysis and obsession with scruples are frowned upon as a morbid state. In placing themselves in antisocial conditions, the ascetics had prepared the return of the new man to history. The complete cycle had been achieved. In its origins placed outside history, monasticism was to become a religious force that would most strongly influence history.

Tradition reestablished the balance in a masterly fashion. After the purification of the desert, the spiritual leaders taught a new and definitive interiorization. "Enter within thy soul and there find God, the angels and the kingdom." [101] "The purified heart becomes an interior heaven." [102] It is no longer by extraordinary conditions of life, but by true prayer that a monk becomes *isangelos,* equal to the angels.[103] The rule of St. Benedict stresses this: "All that one formerly observed through terror and fear of hell, one now keeps through love of Christ." [104]

Prayer participates in universal existence, and "the heart is inflamed with love for every creature" (St. Macarius, St. Isaac).[105]

---

[100] Matt. 12, 45.
[101] St. Macarius, *P.G.,* 34, 776D.
[102] Philotheus the Sinaite, *Chapitres sur la Sobriété,* 1, 4.
[103] Evagrius, *De Oratione,* 113.
[104] Cf. edition of Dom Butler, pp. 31, 40.
[105] Wensinck, *op. cit.,* p. 341.

The new consciousness expanded in the cosmic charity of the saints.

One can take at random some of the vigorous measures used to arrive at a more balanced ascesis. They tempered the excessive and advised against following it, sometimes by the voice of the Councils. The Council of Ancyra threatened to condemn the intransigence of the ascetics who refused to eat vegetables cooked with meat. Cassian declared: "Excessive fasts do as much harm as gluttony." [106] The encratic and gnostic tendencies which despised the flesh and conjugal life were vigorously opposed.

When St. Simon the Stylite put a chain around his foot in order to reduce his movements to what was strictly necessary, Meletius, the Patriarch of Antioch, told him that one could attain immobility just by the will.

A text of the 6th century speaks of Theodulus the Stylite who lived forty-eight years on a pillar. To his naive question about the recompense due him, an angel told him it would be the same as that of the actor of Damas who had given all his fortune to a woman in dire poverty. The *Historia Monachorum* recounts an episode in the life of Paphnutius, the great ascetic. He asked God to show him the perfect men whose equal he had proved himself to be. There followed a vision in which he saw three persons: a brigand who had saved a woman lost in the desert, a village chief who was just and generous to all, a pearl merchant who distributed all his goods to the poor. *The Spiritual Meadow* of John Moschus describes a young monk who did not hesitate to frequent taverns but who kept his heart pure; he was the envy of an old monk who, after passing fifty years at Scete, had not acquired a like purity of heart.

Under the pedagogical guidance of the Church, the teaching of the Gospel was recognized; henceforth acts of charity surpass ascetic exploits and are placed at the very center. The *Apophthegms* tell of a hermit who after forty years in the desert, said to the abbot of a large monastery: "The sun has never seen me eat." The abbot replied: "As for me, it has never seen me in anger."

[106] *Conferences*, II, 16.

St. Basil made a long sojourn with the monks of Egypt and Syria, and later, with St. Gregory of Nazianzen, drew up his two *Monastic Rules* which later inspired St. Benedict. Profoundly impressed by the desert, he was nevertheless aware of his own times and wrote as a Father of the Church. In his vision of the future, he deliberately accorded less importance to renunciation of the world and much more to love of neighbor and the service of mankind. Thus, if monasticism left the world, it was only to bless it from its retreat and to be mindful of it in its incessant prayer. "The perfect man becomes the equal of the apostles . . . He can return to men and tell them what he has seen in God. He can and he ought, in fact, he cannot do otherwise." [107] St. Maximus the Confessor reacted violently against all pessimism of neo-Platonic origin, and the ascesis of St. Isaac the Syrian strikes us with its extreme appreciation of man and of God's creation.

The hesychastic tradition stresses the body's participation in the exercise of the spirit. Its ascesis does not seek suffering and affliction but endurance through abstention, resistance to distractions, and attention of the heart to essentials. The great truth of the Gospel is clearly affirmed: the spiritual man is such entirely, soul and body. For St. Gregory Palamas, this is man's privilege and his superiority over the angels.

In the 10th and 11th centuries, the great Laura of Athos began a very special experiment. Its eschatological atmosphere is expressed in the tradition of the prayer of Jesus and of the light of Thabor. The Gospel narrative telling of the transfiguration shows it as an anticipation of the parousia and of the kingdom, but after pentecost, the light became interior. In rare cases it can manifest itself and be perceived by means of transfigured senses. The man who inwardly or outwardly contemplates it is transmuted; this is because the light is not only the object but the means of his vision. Iconographically, as the nimbus of the saints shows, the corporal luminosity of the saints is ontologically normal.

With his natural but transfigured eyes, the saint contemplates an immaterial light but his visions and his knowledge are granted to

[107] I. Hausherr, "Saint Symeon le N.T.," in *Orientalia Christiana*, XII, p. xxx.

him. They are never a "possession" of the divine. God, in manifesting himself, safeguards his mystery and his total transcendence. If
he accords us a participation in his life and his presence, he hides
himself in his very manifestation. He hides his inaccessible Being.
The hesychastic tradition is very firm on this point: the transcendence of God is not due to man's weakness but to the nature
of God. Unknowable by nature, God is more than God. Even in
uniting himself to man, God remains transcendent to him. Participation in God is participation only in his energies, in his grace;
this is the burning intimacy of his presence. According to St.
Symeon: "God is the more invisible the more he radiates in man's
spirit." This superessential principle of the divine essence conditions human love, its eternal *epektasis,* its tension toward God, of
which St. Gregory of Nyssa speaks.

Tradition rapidly eliminated all imagination, all mystic intoxication with suffering, and imposed the greatest sobriety. Even
ecstasy was held suspect. "When it seems to you that your spirit
is drawn toward the heights by an invisible force, do not put any
faith in it, but oblige yourself to work. By work a monk avoids all
romantic abstraction and exercises charity. Very often one thinks
that it is a spiritual joy, and it is only sensuality aroused by the
enemy; those who have had this experience can distinguish it,"
teaches Gregory the Sinaite.[108] Evagrius said, "Do not desire to see
either evil powers or angels under pain of sinking into madness." [109]

The liturgy offers an efficacious means of filtering out every dis-
ordered emotion. That is why the life of a monk is centered more
and more on psalmody, prayer and prayerful meditation on the
Scriptures. The soul listens to the Word and allows itself to be
penetrated and filled with it. Biblical ontology forms the categories
of emptiness and fullness, absence and communion. Every spiritual
person aspires to the communion that fills him with God, as the
Blessed Virgin or St. Stephen was filled with the Holy Spirit. From
this biblical source comes the patristic definition of theology: *the
experimental way of union with God.* "If you are a theologian, you

[108] *De la vie contemplative,* 10.
[109] *De Oratione,* 114-116.

will truly pray, and if you truly pray, you are a theologian." [110]
This experience of "the sense of God" permits one to transpose into
eucharistic terms the nuptial dwelling of God in man. Man does not
speculate but he changes. This clear-sighted realism of the ascesis
affirms for all times in its essential principle: No ascesis deprived
of love approaches God. "We shall be judged for the evil we have
done but especially for the good we have neglected and for the
fact that we have not loved our neighbor." [111] *The Shepherd* of
Hermas is likewise explicit in declaring that anyone who has
omitted to help a man in spiritual distress will be held responsible
for his loss.[112] At Mount Athos today the old maxims have lost
nothing of their value: "The true monk is the one who in the
present life possesses nothing but Christ." "The one who has in his
heart even a trace of wickedness is unworthy of the charity of
Christ."

Having arrived at the height of the greatest freedom, the hermit
can find the world again since for him it is no longer bewitched. He
can find men and their city again since he has attained to the
charity that urges him to leave his solitude. On this summit "man
no longer condemns the Jews nor the Greeks nor sinners . . . the
interior man looks at all men with a pure eye, and he rejoices then
on account of the entire universe; he desires with his whole heart
only to love and venerate each and every one," says St. Macarius.[113]
As a messenger and a witness, he mixes with the crowd; as a
charismatic, he opens the door of his cell and receives the world.

Contrary to the purely physical ascesis of mortification, the therapeutic art of tradition rehabilitated matter, and in letters of joy
inscribed the paschal message, the destiny of man to eternal life
on all the tombs throughout the world. The eschatological tone of
the ascesis of all times remains.

The soul recognizes God in its avowal of its total powerlessness;
it renounces itself and no longer belongs to itself. This oblation, this
unconditional giving up of oneself, structures contemplative re-

---

[110] Evagrius, *De Oratione,* 60.
[111] St. Maximus the Confessor, *P.G.,* 99, 932C.
[112] *Simil.,* X, 3, 4.
[113] *Homélies.*

ceptivity; it is humility that has become act. "Naked man follows the naked Christ." He keeps himself in expectation and in his soul he awaits the parousia, the coming of Christ. But this soul bears the world of all men. Purified by ascesis, a spiritual man, according to the fine words of St. Gregory Nazianzen, is "the depositary of the divine love of men".[114]

[114] *P.G.*, 35, 593C.

7
Monasticism Interiorized

1. *The Transmission of Witness*

The crisis that monasticism is passing through almost everywhere could suggest the idea that an historic cycle has just come to a close. However, here as elsewhere, we must guard against simplification and distinguish between changeable forms and the permanent principle, between the transmission of the essential message of the Gospel and the appearance of new witnesses.

We can discover a similar transmission in the very origins of monasticism. Since the time of the deacon Stephen, the testimony of blood has been the sign of the highest and most expressive fidelity. The ideal of the martyr, of that glorious company of "the wounded friends of the bridegroom", of those "violent ones who carry away heaven" and in whom "Christ fights in person", makes the first centuries absolutely unique. On his way to his glorious death, St. Ignatius of Antioch confessed: "It is now that I begin to be a true disciple . . . do not hinder me from being born to life." [115] Likewise for St. Polycarp the martyrs are "the images of true charity . . . the captives laden with venerable chains, which are the jewels of the veritable elect of God".[116] This is why Origen made his somewhat cruel remark that a time of peace is propitious to Satan, who steals from Christ his martyrs, and from the Church her glory.

As a living configuration to Christ crucified, the martyr preaches him in giving himself as "a spectacle" to the world, to angels and to men. "Your bodies are pierced by the sword, but never can your spirit be cut off from divine love. Suffering with Christ, you are consumed by the burning coals of the Holy Spirit. Wounded by

[115] Rom. 5, 3-6.
[116] Philipp. III.

111

divine desire, your martyrs, Lord, rejoice in their wounds," sings the Church.[117]

"Can you drink the chalice that I must drink?" our Lord asked the apostles. This formidable question makes martyrdom conformable to the eucharistic chalice; the soul of the martyr bears the presence of Christ in a very special manner. According to an ancient tradition, every martyr at the moment of his death hears the words addressed to the good thief—"This day you shall be with me in paradise"—and enters immediately into the kingdom.

The peaceful existence of the Church, protected by law from the 4th century, will never suffer any diminution in regard to the violence of her message. The Holy Spirit immediately "invented" the "equivalent of martyrdom". In fact, the testimony that the martyrs rendered to "the one thing necessary" passed to monasticism. "The baptism of blood" of the martyrs gave place to "the baptism of ascesis" of the monks. The celebrated *Life of St. Anthony,* written by St. Athanasius, describes this father of monasticism as the first who had attained holiness without tasting martyrdom.[118] Man had fallen to a level below his nature; ascesis elevated him to one above it. The *metanoia* or conversion strengthened the second birth of baptism that brought about the "little resurrection". Even if the body had to await the "great resurrection", the soul was already immortal.

The liturgical texts call the monks "earthly angels and heavenly men". Monastic holiness forms a type of man that is "very similar" to the living icon of God. One can say that at least here, confronted with the world's compromises, the *metanoia,* the complete reversal of all the economy of the human being, its perfect metamorphosis, had succeeded.

The "dreadful" Thebaid, cradle of so many giants of the spirit, the arid and burning desert, was illuminated with their light. These astonishing masters taught the refined art of living the Gospel. In the silence of their cells and caves, in the school of these "theo-didacts" taught by God, the birth of the *new creature* was slowly effected.

---

[117] *Oktoichos,* Greek.
[118] See D. H. Leclercq, "Monachisme," in *D.A.L.,* XI, 1802.

2. *The Universal Character of Spiritual Monasticism*

Father Florovsky recalls that "too often one forgets the provisory character of monasticism. St. John Chrysostom declared that monasteries are necessary because the world is not Christian. Let it be converted, and the need of a monastic separation will disappear".[119] History has not justified St. John's optimism. Monasticism will surely keep its unique testimony to the end of the world.

However, the baptized world is sufficiently Christian to hear the monastic message and to assimilate it in its own way. This is the whole problem. As formerly, martyrdom was transmitted to the monastic institution, so likewise today, it seems, monasticism creates a certain receptivity in the universal priesthood of the laity. The testimony of the Christian faith in the framework of the modern world postulates the universal vocation of *interiorized monasticism*.

Past history gives us two solutions. The first, that of monasticism, preaches a complete separation from a society that lives according to "the elements of this world", and from its economic, political and sociological problems. This is "the flight to the desert", and later the autonomous existence of communities that care for all the needs of their members. The "monastic republic" of Mount Athos is a striking example of social autarchic life, separated from the world and even opposed to it. It is perfectly clear that since everybody cannot share this vocation, the monastic solution remains limited; it is not the solution for the world in its totality.

The second solution tried to Christianize the world without leaving it in order to build the Christian city. The theocracies, in the East as well as in the West, manifest this effort under the ambiguous forms of empires and Christian States. The resounding failure of this attempt proves that one can never impose the Gospel from above, nor prescribe grace as a law.

Is there a third solution? Without prejudging, one can at least say that this third ought to appropriate the two others in making

[119] "Le Corps du Christ vivant," in *La Sainte Eglise universelle*.

them interior, that is, in applying their principles to something beyond their precise forms. "You are not of this world, you are in the world." These words of the Lord recommend a very special ministry, that of being a sign, a reference to "the wholly other". Formerly it was realized differently. At present it seems to show itself above the "desert" and the "city", for it is called to surpass every form in order to express itself everywhere and in all circumstances.

The West has regarded monasticism and the lay state as two forms of life; one responding to the counsels, the other, to the precepts of the Gospel. The unique absolute is then broken. On one side, the perfect advance; on the other, the weak stand, living by half measures. Certain ascetics justified conjugal life only because it brings forth virgins and peoples convents.

The fundamentally homogeneous character of Eastern spirituality ignores the difference between "the precepts" and "the evangelical counsels". It is in its total requirement that the Gospel addresses itself to all and everyone.

"When Christ," says St. John Chrysostom, "orders us to follow the narrow path, he addresses himself to all men. The monk and the lay person must attain the same heights." [120] We can see indeed that there exists only one spirituality for all without distinction as to its exigency, whether for bishop, monk, or lay person, and this is the monastic spirituality.[121] Now this has been formed by lay-monks, which gives to the term "lay" an extremely spiritual and ecclesial meaning.

In fact, according to the great teachers, the monks were only those who wished "to be saved", those who "led a life according to the Gospel", "sought the one thing necessary", and "did violence to themselves in all things".[122] It is quite evident that these words define exactly the state of every believing lay person. St. Nil thought all monastic practices were required of people of the world.[123] As St. John Chrysostom said: "Those who live in the world, even

[120] *In Epist. ad Haeb.*, 7, 4; 7, 41; *Adv. oppugn. vitae monast.*, 3, 14.
[121] Cf. Pourrat, *La Spiritualité chrétienne*, I, ix.
[122] St. Nil, *P.G.*, 79, 180D.
[123] *Epist.* I, 167, 169.

though married, ought to resemble the monks in everything else. You are entirely mistaken if you think that there are some things required of seculars, and others for monks . . . they will have the same account to render." [124] Prayer, fasting, the reading of Scripture and ascetic discipline are imposed on all by the same prescription. St. Theodore of Studium in his letter to a Byzantine dignitary drew up the program of monastic life and specified: "Do not believe that this list is of value only for a monk and not *entirely and equally for a lay person.*" [125]

When the Fathers spoke, they addressed themselves to all the members of the mystical body, without any distinction between clergy and laity; they spoke to the universal priesthood. The actual pluralism of the theologies of the episcopate, the clergy, religious and the laity, being unknown at the time of the Fathers, would be even incomprehensible to them. The Gospel in its entirety is applicable to every particular problem in any environment.

On the other hand, certain great figures among the monks show clearly that they went beyond their own state, as well as beyond every formula or definite form. Such, for example, was the luminous figure of St. Seraphin of Sarov. He did not form disciples nor was he master of any school; however, he is the master of all, for his testimony to the Orthodox Church surpasses all that is a type, category, style, definition or limit. His paschal joy did not come from his temperament, but is the echo of Orthodoxy itself. With ordinary language he said extraordinary things that he had received from the Holy Spirit. After a fearful struggle, shadowed by a silence that hid a life that no monk could endure, St. Seraphin left the extreme practices of the hermits and stylites and went into the world. "An earthly angel and a heavenly man", he transcended even monasticism. In a certain measure, he was no longer a monk retired from the world nor a man living among men; he was both, and in surpassing both, he was essentially a witness to the Holy Spirit. He said this in his famous conversation with Nicolas Motovilov: "It is not to you alone that it has been given to understand these things, but by you to the whole world, in order that you may

124 *Hom. in Epist. ad Haeb.*, 7, 41.
125 *P.G.*, 99, 1388.

be strengthened in the work of God for the utility of many others. *As to the fact that you are a lay person and that I am a monk, there is no need to think of that* . . . The Lord seeks hearts filled with love for God and their neighbor. This is the throne on which he loves to sit and on which he will appear in the fullness of his heavenly glory. 'My child, give me your heart, and all the rest I shall likewise give you', because it is in the heart of man that the kingdom of God exists . . . The Lord hears the prayers of the monk as well as those of a simple lay person, provided that *both* have a faith without error, are truly believers and love God from the depths of their hearts, for even 'if their faith is only a grain of mustard seed, *both* of them will move mountains." [126] Both, the monk and the lay person, are a sign and a reference to "the wholly other". St. Tikhon of Zadonsk wrote in the same vein to ecclesiastical authorities: "Do not be in a hurry to multiply the monks. The black habit does not save. The one who wears a white habit and has the spirit of obedience, humility, and purity, he is a true monk of *interiorized monasticism.*" [127]

The monasticism that was entirely centered on the last things formerly changed the face of the world. Today it makes an appeal to all, to the laity as well as to the monks, and it points out a universal vocation. For each one, it is a question of adaptation, of a personal equivalent of the monastic vows.

3. *The Three Temptations, the Lord's Three Answers, and the Three Monastic Vows*

The three monastic vows constitute a great charter of human liberty. *Poverty* frees from the ascendancy of the material; it is the baptismal transmutation into the new creature. *Chastity* frees from the ascendancy of the carnal; it is the nuptial mystery of the agape. *Obedience* frees from the idolatry of the ego; it indicates the son-

---

[126] The revelations of St. Seraphin of Sarov, French translation in *Le Semeur* (April, 1927).

[127] Anna Guippius, *Saint Tykhone de Zadonsk* (Paris), p. 15, in Russian edition.

ship to the Father. All, whether monks or not, ask God for these things in the tripartite structure of the Lord's prayer: *obedience* to the will of the Father; *poverty* of one who is hungry only for the substantial and eucharistic bread; *chastity,* the purification from evil.

In Old Testament days, each time that the Israelites, as nomadic pilgrims, encountered the material civilization of "the settled countries", they discovered there three temptations: idols, contrary to *obedience;* prostitution, contrary to *chastity;* wealth, contrary to *poverty.* The prophets did not cease from denouncing and fighting the primacy of efficiency over truth, material success and its power as the standard of value, and justification of everything by force. Today's world has adopted these principles more than ever before. Formerly all the efforts of the prophets were directed against them; they preached *adoration* of the one God, the *purification* of the people, the exercise of *charity* toward the poor.

The New Testament, in the account of the Lord's three temptations, takes up the same subject, but now under the form of a supreme and definitive revelation. The text stresses this: "When the devil had tried every temptation, he departed from him." [128] The Servant of Yahweh, the *obedient* man, the *poor* man, who had "no place to lay his head", the *pure* man—"Behold, Satan has nothing in me"—went to the heart of the desert as the prototype of the monk, and proclaimed *urbi et orbi* the triple synthesis of human existence.

Patristic thought attributes to this account a central place among the first events of the Gospel. Christ had come to fight against the evil powers that were enslaving men, and it is this liberating quality of his work that is in question here. St. Justin [129] compared the temptations of the first and second Adam and showed in Christ the universal attitude of every son of God. Likewise, Origen saw here a decisive event that enlightens the final combat of all the faithful, for what is at stake is, neither more nor less, "to make every man a martyr or an idolator".[130] He underlines the

---

[128] Luke 4, 13.
[129] *Dialogue avec Triphon,* 103, 6.
[130] *Ad. Mart.,* 32.

fact that the temptations sought to make of Christ a new source of sin, since its scope would put it on the level of original sin. For St. Irenaeus,[131] the temptation failed to make man definitely captive, and consequently the brilliant victory of Jesus orients the combat of the Church and frees the true follower from all satanic ascendancy. "I have given you power to tread . . . over all the might of your enemies." [132]

Thus the thought of the Fathers from the beginning saw in the account of the temptations in the desert, the *ultima verba* of the Gospel message. Indeed to the archetype of man in the divine wisdom, the tempter opposed his counterplan, the man of demoniacal wisdom. St. Paul even mentions a demoniacal pentecost (2 Corinthians 11, 4). All human history unfolds in a striking summary where everything is unsettled in one way or another. Satan advances three infallible solutions of human destiny: the alchemist *miracle* of the philosopher's stone; the *mystery* of occult sciences and their boundless powers; and finally, one unifying *authority*.

To transform stones into bread [133] is to solve the economic problem, to suppress "the sweat of man's brow", all ascetic efforts, and creation itself. To cast oneself down from the temple is to suppress the temple and even the need of prayer; it is to substitute magic power for God, to triumph over the principle of necessity, and to solve the *problem of knowledge*. Now knowledge without limits causes the submission of cosmic and carnal elements, the immediate satisfaction of all covetousness, a duration made up of "little eternities of enjoyment", the destruction of chastity. Finally, to unite all nations by the power of a single weapon is to solve the *political* problem, suppress war and inaugurate the era of the peace of this world.

The first act took place between the God-Man and Satan. If Christ had prostrated himself before Satan, Satan would have retired from the world, because there would be nothing for him to do there.

[131] *Adv. Haer.*, V, 20, 2.
[132] Luke 10, 19.
[133] It is to make "bread without sweat".

Definitely captive, humanity would live without knowing the freedom of choice, for it would never attain to good or evil.

Temptation would weigh once again and weigh heavily in the prayer of our Lord: "Father, if it is possible, let this cup pass away from me." [134] What the Father did not do, Satan could do, and he offered the very real possibility of definitively withdrawing the cup and escaping the cross. The tragedy of God and of man would then have been resolved in a demoniacal "happy ending".

We must take an exact measure of the adversary and grasp the scope of the evil that obliges God to leave "the summit of silence", and to utter the cry: "Why hast thou forsaken me?" It makes temptation very real, without adding anything fictitious or any stage setting. In leaving Lucifer's will free to pervert himself into the evil one, God has asked himself the question of being or of not being the *unique,* at the risk of finding himself a being by himself, suffering and abandoned. To the God entered in time, Satan proposed an infallible messiahship that would have no risk of suffering, and that would be founded on a triple suppression of freedom, on a triple slavery of man: the violation of his freedom by miracle, mystery and power.[135]

The divine refusal changed nothing in the disposition of the tempter. His project is now being offered to man, and it is this second act that conditions history.

The cruel times of the persecutions force one to salute the Christian empire. The paradoxical canonization of Constantine, declared "a saint", bears witness to the positive element of his gesture, justified dialectically by the principle of "economy". The Church was imposed on the pagan world; it obtained a wide hearing; is it going to succeed? This is another question. In this confrontation, one party is going "to soil its hands", another will keep them clean from the compromise; both are necessary and both complement each other. Moreover, it was not the official and functionalized Church that spoke the words of life; it confided this

[134] Matt. 26, 39.
[135] This aspect of the three temptations is at the center of "The Legend of the Great Inquisitor" of Dostoievski.

task to the fathers of the Councils, and above all to those great
spiritual men, the monks. The importance of the coming of monasticism is in the liberty of spirit that the irregular formation of
charismatics will enjoy on the margin of the world and the established Church.

We must admit that the empire proclaimed Christian was built
on the three solutions of Satan, certainly not entirely nor consciously, but in mingling light with darkness, God and Caesar, the
suggestions of Satan and the refutations of Christ. The empire was
ambiguous, for it twisted the cross; no "Christian State" as a
State has ever been a crucified State. It is on the subject of the
Church that John of Saroug asks the question: "What bride has
ever chosen a crucified as spouse?" On the contrary, misunderstanding about the protective power of the cross delivers princes
and politicians without defense to the three temptations. Constantine founded an empire whose greatness and prosperity were
more dangerous than the cruelties of Nero.

It was at this moment that monasticism entered upon the stage
of history. It is the most categorical *no* to all compromise, to all
conformity, to all cooperation with the tempter, disguised now by
the imperial crown, now by the episcopal miter. It is the resounding
yes to the Christ of the desert. One can never insist enough on the
salvific character of monasticism. "Our Lord has left us as a heritage
what he himself has done when he was tempted by Satan," said
Evagrius.[136] From its origin, Egyptian monasticism understood its
spirituality as the continuation of the fight begun by the Lord in
the desert.

*If the empire made its secret temptation out of Satan's three
invitations, monasticism was openly built on Christ's three immortal
answers.* It is astonishing that no exegesis has ever recognized the
triple word placed as a cornerstone in the very being of monasticism. *The three monastic vows reproduce exactly the three answers of Jesus.* Christ as *monk* fulfilled them in accepting the cup
and in mounting the cross "that he might destroy the works of the
devil".[137] "Cancelling the decree against us which was hostile to us.

[136] *Antirrhétique* (ed. Frankenberg), p. 472.
[137] 1 John 3, 8.

Indeed, he has taken it completely away, nailing it to the cross." [138]

Christ destroyed the satanic plan of triple slavery, and from the summit of the cross he announced the divine charter of triple freedom. St. Paul emphasizes this by his energetic warning in the passage that begins with "see that no one deceives you",[139] or takes away that freedom of which the cross is the dazzling pledge. Every monk is a *staurophore* (a cross-bearer). He is also a *pneumatophore* (Spirit-bearer), for the cross is the triumphant power of the Holy Spirit manifesting Christ crucified. "Give your blood and receive the Spirit", is an ancient monastic saying which reveals that in every monk freedom takes flesh by the action of the Holy Spirit. Such were the first charismatics before democratization was made necessary by the crowds of monks, and before the need of organizing them led to the imposition of harsh monastic law. Those who knew how to make this law a source of grace corresponded to the authentic grandeur of monasticism. Above every organized institution, this remained essentially an *event*.

Christ's three answers resounded in the silence of the desert; it was therefore here that the monks came in order to hear them again and to receive them as the rule of their monastic life, *under the form of the three vows*.

St. Gregory Palamas describes the type of holy monks thus: "They have given up the enjoyment of material goods (poverty), human glory (obedience), and the evil pleasures of the body (chastity), and they have preferred an evangelical life; thus the perfect have arrived at the adult age according to Christ." [140] In a letter to Paul Asen on the subject of clothes and exterior signs of the monastic degrees, St. Gregory counseled "to perfect the manner of life and not the changing of clothes". In the great figures of monasticism we see how they went beyond every formal principle and every form; they passed from symbols to reality.

"I will lead her into the desert and speak to her heart." [141] This "advance of one alone toward the only one", shows the primacy

---

[138] Col. 2, 14.
[139] Col. 2, 8.
[140] *P.G.*, 150, 1228.
[141] Hos. 2, 16.

of the anchorhold and hermitage over the cenobitic form; it indicates an aristocracy of the spirit that frees itself from everything, even from a community and its rules. However, if one leaves society to find freedom, it is in order to find the world of men again and in a better way.

This level of freedom transcends the limits of institutions, and in it can be seen its universal significance as a solution of human destiny. The interiorized monasticism of the royal priesthood finds its own spirituality in taking to itself the equivalent of the monastic vows.

Formerly fidelity implied the blood of martyrs or the exploits of the desert, striking spectacles in their visible grandeur. At the moment when the Constantinian epoch definitely ended, the combat of the Christian king gave way to the martyrdom [142] and the heroism of the faithful in their daily life, which is not necessarily spectacular.

4. *The Vow of Poverty in the Interior Monasticism of the Laity*

Our Lord's answer: "Not by bread alone does man live, but by every word that comes forth from the mouth of God," indicates the passage from the old curse: "In the sweat of your brow you shall eat bread," to the new hierarchy of values, to the primacy of spirit over matter, of grace over necessity. In the house of Martha and Mary, Jesus passed from the material repast and physical hunger to the spiritual banquet, to hunger of the one thing necessary. The version of the beatitudes in St. Luke's Gospel accentuates the reversal of situations: "Blessed are the poor . . . those who hunger." Even physical poverty "in the sweat of your brow" is no longer a curse, but a sign of election placed on the humble, the last and the least, as opposed to the rich and powerful. The "poor of Israel" available for the kingdom, and more generally "the poor in spirit", receive as a gift, gratuitously, "the wheat of angels", the Word of God in the eucharistic bread.

If the stones mentioned in the temptation had become bread, this miracle would have expelled "the poor man" above all, not

[142] Apoc. 20.

the beggar who is the object of charity bazaars, but the poor one who shares his *being,* his eucharistic flesh and blood. Thus, does every truly poor person "in the sweat of his heart" share his being. Such a poverty was preached by the Fathers of the Church of the type of St. John Chrysostom. The Gospel requires what no political doctrine would demand from its adherents. On the world scale, only an economy based on need and not on profit has any chance of succeeding, but it entails sacrifices and renunciation. One cannot enjoy material goods with a total absence of order. True needs vary according to vocations, but the essential principle is found in independence in regard to all possessions.

Absence of the need to have becomes a need not to have. The disinterested freedom of the spirit in regard to things restores its capacity of loving them as gifts from God. To live in what is "given in addition" is to live between destitution and the superfluous. However, the monastic ideal does not preach formal poverty but a wise frugality of needs.

The measure of poverty, which is always very personal, requires a creative inventiveness and excludes all sectarian spirit. The problem is not in the privation but in the use; it is the quality of gift that one puts in the proffered glass of water that justifies man at the last judgment. This is why St. James makes clear the meaning of alms: "Give aid to orphans and widows in their tribulation." [143] If there is nothing to be shared, there remains the example of the unjust steward of the Gospel parable who distributes the goods of his master (inexhaustible love) in order to win friendships in Christ.

He who possesses nothing becomes, like St. Symeon the New Theologian, "the poor brother of everybody". Simeon, Anna, Joseph and Mary were "the poor of Israel" looking for the consolation of Israel, but they were already rich in God, for the Holy Spirit was upon them.[144] Thus the Blessed Virgin kept all these things in her heart, made them her very self, and the Holy Spirit made of her "the Gift of Consolation" and "the Gate to the Kingdom".

[143] James 1, 27.
[144] Luke 2, 25.

5. *The Vow of Chastity*

"Thou shalt not tempt the Lord thy God." To tempt is to try. To tempt God means to try the limits of his magnanimity. Has he not created man "in his image", almost "a micro-god"? "You are all gods, sons of the Most High." Conscious of his greatness, this "little god" dares to claim the attributes of his high dignity. To tempt the Lord in this case is to make use of God, of the power equal to that of God, in order to satisfy all his desires.

In the second temptation [145]—to cast himself down from the top of the temple—there is no question of the exploit of Icarus. The latter was only a symbol of domination over the cosmic elements. The temptation here is to covet the much vaster power to which St. Luke refers when he writes: [146] "I have given you power to tread upon serpents and scorpions, and over all the might of the enemy; and nothing shall hurt you." This power includes domination over space; to throw oneself down from the roof of the temple would be to overcome earth's gravity and to rule the heavens. "Do not rejoice in this, that the spirits are subject to you (the submission of which Satan speaks); rejoice rather in this, that your names are written in heaven." The name designates the person. The text speaks of the joy of seeing oneself admitted into the spiritual heaven of the divine presence. We see here the message of the freedom of the children of God and of their heavenly power as opposed to all temptation by the power of earthly magic.

In the hands of "leaders", this magic power arouses the collective passions of crowds; it hypnotizes, charms and dominates. For everyone this magic means the power over space and all that it contains on the material plane. It violates the mystery of nature, profanes the sacredness of the cosmos, the creation of God.

We must remember the close relationship between woman and the cosmos. The whole gamut of pagan mysteries prefigured this even up to the cult of the Virgin Mary—"Blessed Land, Promised

[145] Matt. 4, 6.
[146] Luke 10, 19-20.

Land, Abundant Harvest." These liturgical names are the cosmic symbols of the new Eve—*Virgin and Mother*. This mysterious bond explains the command not to tempt God, not to sully and profane *chastity*. This virtue goes beyond the physiological and expresses the entire and chaste structure of the human spirit. It constitutes the charism of the sacrament of marriage. In a wider sense, it inspires the meaning of the sacredness of every particle of God's creation, inviolable in its expectation of salvation that is to come from the chaste man.[147] The power of chastity is the contrary of the power of magic and signifies the return to the true "supernaturally natural power" of paradise.[148] "Thou shalt not tempt thy God" means then that you shall not make of your conformity to God the accomplice of your passions in anti-chastity.

Origen speaks of the "chastity of the soul" [149] which the Fathers of the desert called "the purification of the heart". Even those monks who were already married attained this spiritual development. There was already a transcendence of the physiological state itself.

Chaste love is attracted by the heart that remains virgin beyond every corporeal actuation. According to the Bible, there is a total "knowledge" of two beings, a conversation of spirit with spirit in which the body seems amazingly the vehicle of the spiritual. This is why St. Paul says that man should learn "to possess his vessel in holiness and honor".[150] As undefiled matter suitable for liturgical use, the chaste man is entirely, body and soul, the matter of the *sacrament* of marriage, with the sanctification of his love. The charism of the sacrament effects the transcendence of the self toward the transparent presence of one for the other, of one toward the other, in order to offer themselves together as a single being to God.

Chastity—σωφροσύνη—integrates all the elements of the human being into a whole that is virginal and interior as to the spirit, and that is why St. Paul speaks of the salvation of every mother by

[147] See Rom. 8, 21.
[148] According to Clement of Alexandria, the sacrament of marriage brings "a paradisal grace". *P.G.*, 8, 1096.
[149] *P.G.*, 12, 728C.
[150] 1 Thess. 4, 4.

means of chastity.[151] The Pauline dialectic of the circumcision of the flesh interiorizes it even to "the circumcised . . . heart".[152] The same dialectic interiorizes chastity: "He who is not spiritual in his flesh becomes carnal even in his spirit," and again, "the virginity of the flesh belongs to a small number, the virginity of the heart should belong to all." [153]

Love penetrates to the very root of instinct and "changes even the substance of things", says St. John Chrysostom.[154] It raises the empirical aims to the ends created by the spirit, and makes of them a pure source of immaterial joy.

Familiarity with icons purifies the imagination, teaches "the mortification of the eyes" in order to contemplate beauty chastely. In the beauty of the body, the soul is its form, and in the beauty of the soul, the image of God delights us. Islamic wisdom has understood this, as can be seen in the saying: "The paradise of the faithful gnostic is his own body, and the hell of the man without faith or gnosis is equally his own body." [155]

Bishop Nonnus of Edessa in contemplating the beauty of a dancer (the future St. Pelagia) "took it as a subject for glorifying the sovereign beauty, of which her beauty was only the reflection, and feeling himself transported by the fire of divine love, shed tears of joy . . . He was raised", continues St. John Climacus, "to a wholly incorruptible state before the universal resurrection." [156]

An erotic imagination decomposes the spirit by an unextinguishable thirst of hell. On the contrary, the sign of chastity, according to St. Clement of Rome, is when a man, looking at a woman, has no carnal thought in his mind. "O singular woman, you are the entire species for me," says the poet of the unique woman in singing of chaste conjugal love.

The history of Tobias admirably describes the victory over concupiscence. The angel's name, Raphael, signifies "the remedy of

[151] 1 Tim. 2, 15.
[152] Rom. 2, 26-29.
[153] St. Augustine, *Enarr. in Ps.* 147.
[154] *P.G.,* 61, 273.
[155] See H. Corbin, *Terre céleste et corps de résurrection,* p. 161.
[156] *P.G.,* 88, 893.

God"; it is the chastity that is present in every great love when it is lighted by the "blazing fire of the Eternal".[157]

Berdyaev clearly describes this inward chastity: "Love is called upon to conquer the 'old' and to discover a new flesh in which the union of two is not a loss but an accomplishment of virginity, that is, of its entirely new integrality. In this incandescent point the transfiguration of the world uniquely can begin." [158]

"To throw himself from the pinnacle of the temple" [159] means to alienate himself and to render himself useless. The answer to this temptation and to the concupiscence that inclines a man to seize the power that Christ really possesses to the point of governing even the angels, is chastity. "To cast himself down" designates the movement from the high to the low, from heaven to hell; this was Lucifer's exact itinerary and that of the fall of man that brought concupiscence. Chastity is an ascension; it is the Savior's itinerary, from hell to the Father's kingdom. It is also an inward ascension toward the burning presence of God.

It is within one's mind that one throws himself into the presence of God, and chastity is only one of the names of the nuptial mystery of the lamb.

6. *The Vow of Obedience*

"Thou shalt adore the Lord thy God and him only shalt thou worship." The liturgical definition of man, the being of the *Trisagion* and the *Sanctus,* suppresses all passive states. True obedience to God implies the supreme freedom that is always creative. Christ shows this in his manner of accomplishing every law; he fulfills and raises the law to his own mysterious truth of being grace. Likewise the negative and restrictive form of the decalogue—"Thou

---

[157] Cf. Canticle of Canticles, 8, 6.

[158] *Destin de l'homme* (Paris), p. 260, in Russian edition.

[159] The treatise *Beracot* of Talmud of Babylon (fol. 55) contains the following passage: "The one who climbs in a dream onto a roof will climb to greatness; the one who comes down from a roof will come down from greatness." Satan's secret desire is to make the Son come down from the summit of divine greatness.

shalt not"—is fulfilled in giving place to the beatitudes, to the positive and limitless creation of holiness.

Obedience in the Gospel is receptive of truth, and the latter sets one free. This is why God does not issue orders, but he utters appeals and invitations: "Listen, Israel." "If anyone wills. . . ." "If you wish to be perfect. . . ." It is an invitation to find freedom again: "If anyone wishes to come to me and does not hate his . . ."—the possessive adjective here indicates a captive state, and "hate" means to free oneself from it in order to find the true unpossessive charity.

The teaching that comes from the school of "spiritual fathers" is enlightening. They warn of the great danger that one runs in seeking an aid. The greater the authority of a father, the greater should be his self-effacement. A disciple can indeed formulate the true and only aim of his request: "Father, tell me what the Holy Spirit suggests to you in order to heal my soul." [160] Abbot Poëmen on his side specifies the art of a staret: "Never command, but be for all an example, never a lawgiver." [161] A young man once went to an old ascetic to be instructed in the way of perfection, but the old man did not say a word. The other asked him the reason for his silence. "Am I then a superior to command you?" he answered. "I shall say nothing. Do, if you want, *what you see me do.*" From then on the young man imitated the old ascetic in everything and learned the meaning of silence and of free obedience.[162]

A spiritual father is never "a director of conscience"; he is before all else a charismatic. He does not engender *his* spiritual son, he engenders a son of God. Both, *in common*, place themselves in the school of truth. The disciple receives the gift of spiritual attention, the father receives that of being the organ of the Holy Spirit. St. Basil advises to find "a friend of God", who gives the certitude that God speaks through him. "Call no one father" means that all fatherhood shares in the fatherhood of God, that all obedience is obedience to the Father's will in sharing in the acts of the obedient Christ.

---

[160] *Apophtegmata Patrum.*
[161] *P.G.,* 65, 363; 65, 564.
[162] *P.G.,* 65, 224.

John of Lycopolis counsels: "Judge your thoughts piously according to God; if you cannot, ask one who is *capable* of judging them." [163] The aim is to destroy the wall that desires have raised between the soul and God. To those who have practiced the art of humility, Theognostus says: "The one who has exercised submission and spiritual obedience and has made his body subject to his spirit, has no need of any submission to a man. He is subject to the Word of God and to his law, as a truly obedient man." [164] And again: "He who wishes to dwell in the desert ought not to need being instructed; he ought to be himself a teacher, otherwise he will suffer . . ."[165] However, this is for the strong. The advice explains the essential—no obedience to human elements, no idolatry of a spiritual father, even if he is a saint. Every counsel of a staret leads a man to a state of freedom before the face of God.

Obedience crucifies man's own will in order to arouse the final freedom—the spirit listening to the Holy Spirit.

7. *Christian Liberty and Monastic Freedom*

When there have been historic deformations, they have betrayed the magnificent type of monk, a man absolutely free in the service of his king.[166] They have made him a being that has been broken by submission to harsh laws.

If since the Middle Ages we remark a divorce between mystic spirituality and theology, *the world of today has need of saints who have genius,* in order to find again the unity of prayer and dogma. For the Fathers of the Church: "A theologian is one who knows how to pray." "For those who are not capable of receiving the burning rays of Christ, the saints are there to furnish them with a light; this latter is very inferior, but since they are scarcely capable of receiving it, it is sufficient to fill them." [167]

---

163 See *Recherches de science religieuse,* 41 (1953), p. 526.
164 *Philocalie,* I, p. 500.
165 *Vitae Patrum,* VII, 19, 6.
166 Mark the Ascetic declares: "After baptism, the exploit of every Christian is solely the affair of his faith and of his freedom" (*P.G.,* 65, 985).
167 Origen, *In Joann.,* I, I, 25.

He who builds his life on the three monastic vows does so also on the three replies of Christ. By these three vows a Christian does not bind himself; he frees himself. He can then turn to the world and tell what he has seen in God. If he has learned how to grow to the stature of "the new man", of the adult in Christ, the world will listen to him.

The one who *knows* because his faith sees the invisible; the one who can raise the dead, if God wishes it, because he already lives "the little resurrection"; the one who can glimpse the *meaning* because he can put the true name on everything, having the name of Jesus "attached" as it were to his every breath—this one can inaugurate the latter times and announce the parousia.

The division of Christianity is not at all an obstacle, but a lack of the true freedom that has its origin in total truth. More than anyone else, monks can bring about this unity because they would do it *liturgically*. Their "orthodoxy" does not harden anything into interdicts; it lays all the pathways open. In their adoration and songs of praise, they exclude nobody; they invite each and every one to become "adult" in Christ. Such maturity places one in a position beyond distorted situations in the body of Christ on the level of the one and only.

According to the fine words of St. Symeon the New Theologian, the Holy Spirit fears no one and despises no one. As an image of the Holy Spirit, monasticism is a living ecumenical "epiklesis". Unity can be found only in this dimension of universal monasticism, if the latter knows how to make itself as free as the breath of the **Holy Spirit**.

8
The Human Being

The Bible knows nothing of the Greek dualism of flesh and mind in conflict, of the body being the prison of the soul. It knows only the moral struggle between the desire of the creator and the desires of the creature, between the standard—holiness—and sin-perversion, but in this conflict the entire man is engaged. Thus, the opposition between *the animal man and the spiritual man* has reference to the totality of the human being. According to St. Augustine, man is carnal even in his spirit or he is spiritual even in his flesh.

The soul vivifies the body and makes of it a living flesh; the spirit spiritualizes and makes of them both a spiritual man. The spirit does not place the soul and body side by side, but it manifests itself through the psychic and the corporeal in qualifying them by its energies. In accordance with this structure of the human being, asceticism constitutes a very exact science and a vast culture that renders the body and the soul transparent and submissive to the spiritual. On the other hand, man can "extinguish the spirit",[168] cause the source of his life to dry up, have carnal thoughts and reduce himself to animal flesh, the prey of death and hell.

The biblical vision thus permits us to take an exact measure of evil and to discover its secret origins. Sin never comes from below, from the flesh, but from above, from the spirit. The first fall occurred in the world of angels, pure spirits.

Carnal perversion denounces and accuses the *sin of the spirit against the flesh.* That is why chastity transcends physiology alone and depends upon the entire structure of the spirit. The emptiness of a roaming and decentralized spirit causes dispersion of its energies. On the contrary, spiritual writers teach the silence of the heart, "the language of the future world", and the recollection that

[168] 1 Thess. 5, 19.

131

is opposed to all dissipation of thought. They seek inwardness saying: "Do not seek anything outside, but enter within yourself, into your heart, and there find God, the angels, and the kingdom."

The heart of which the Bible speaks does not coincide, however, with the emotional center of which the psychologists speak. The Jews thought with their hearts. As a metaphysical center, it integrates all the faculties of the human being; reason, intuition, will, are never strangers to the choices and sympathies of the heart. Radiating and penetrating everywhere, it is nevertheless hidden in its own mysterious depths. "Know thyself" is addressed above all to this secret heart.

"Who can understand the heart," Jeremiah asks, and he immediately answered, "I, the Lord, alone probe the mind and test the heart." [169] This means God alone can penetrate to the obscure sphere of the unconscious and subconscious. St. Peter also speaks of "the inner life of the heart"; [170] and it is at this unfathomable depth that the human ego keeps itself. St. Gregory of Nyssa clearly indicated this depth, showing it to be in the image of God: "Man, in his *unknowability* of himself, manifests the imprint of the ineffable." [171]

"Where thy treasure is, there also will thy heart be." [172] Man is worth what the desires of his heart, the objects of his love, are worth. "The prayer of Jesus", called "the prayer of the heart", makes the heart the place of his presence, "for God has put into the human heart the desire for him".[173] To find in God the absolutely desirable and to place one's heart there reveals an astonishing intimacy with God. Indeed, the Gospel places above the morality of slaves and mercenaries that of *the friends of God*. "No longer do I call you servants . . . But I have called you friends," [174] Christ said. God does even more in asking man to accomplish his will as if it were man's own will. In saying "Thy will be done", we say, "I desire it, it is my will that

---

[169] Jer. 17, 9-10.
[170] 1 Peter 3, 4.
[171] *P.G.*, 44, 155.
[172] Matt. 6, 21.
[173] St. Gregory of Nyssa, *P.G.*, 44, 801A.
[174] John 15, 15.

thine be done." Such a harmony between the two *fiats* raises the human person to the level of the heart of God.

The Latin word *persona* as well as the Greek *prosopon* signifies "mask", and contains a profound philosophy of the human person. To exist is to participate in being or in nothingness. Man can make of himself "an icon of God" or he can become a demoniacal grimace, an ape of God. "He who is near me is near the fire," declares an ancient agraphon; [175] the one who understands it "does not cease adding fire to fire".[176] Man can revive the flame of love or the fire of Gehenna. He can convert his *yes* into an infinity of unions; he can also by his *no* break his being into infernal separations and solitudes.

Created to the image and likeness of God, man possesses an essential orientation that determines him. The resemblance proposed is in the personal realization of the objective image. It releases the *epektasis,* the tension of striving toward the Most High. As every copy is attracted by its original, man as an image aspires to go beyond himself in order to cast himself into God and to find there the appeasement of his nostalgia. Holiness is nothing else but an unquenchable thirst, an intensity of desire, for God. By its light the ascesis of spiritual attention learns the inestimable art of seeing everything as an image of God. "A perfect monk," says St. Nil of Sinai, "will esteem after God all men as God himself." [177] This iconographic manner of looking at every man explains the great ascetics' astonishing optimism, the striking tone of their joy, their authentically evangelical appreciation of man; they always showed an infinite respect for man as "the place of God".

We can understand the scope of the *Ave* in the salutation that St. Seraphin used to address to all whom he met, "My joy". He saw God himself coming to meet him; he read his love on every face, and joyously saluted his presence.[178]

A created incarnate spirit, man is placed between the spirituality of the angels and the carnal corporeality of this world. St. Gregory

[175] A. Resch. *Agrapha,* 150.

[176] St. John Climacus, *The Heavenly Ladder, P.G.,* 88, 644A.

[177] See Evagrius, *De Oratione,* 123.

[178] See our study, "St. Seraphin of Sarov," in *The Ecumenical Review* (April, 1963).

of Palamas saw in this situation the primacy of man over the angels. The angels are "the second lights", reflecting the light of God. Man is *transmuted* into light and illumines the world. "You are the light of the world." The nimbus of the saints shows this. The cosmic nature of the world as well as his own body is the biosphere of the human spirit. As artist and creator, it is with these elements that he is called upon to create the values of the kingdom, and this is why the angels serve him.

9
The Ascesis of the Spiritual Life

"Put on the armor of God, that you may be able to stand against the wiles of the devil." [179] St. Paul exhorts all the faithful to exercise themselves in the combats of the faith and gives us an image taken from military life and from that of sports—the soldier and the athlete.

The word "ascesis" comes from the Greek *akesis* and means exercise, effort, exploit. One can speak of the athletic ascesis when it seeks to render the body supple, obedient, resistant to every obstacle. The ascesis of scientists and doctors shows their magnificent abnegation that sometimes costs them their lives.

Monastic tradition has given to this term a very precise meaning; it designates the interior combat necessary in order that the spiritual acquire a mastery over the material.

Among the first monks, there were some called messalians, who had the notion of forming an aristocracy of super-Christians. Tradition, especially that of St. Basil, has always rejected this false conception. In his works, St. Basil hesitated to use the word "monk" on account of these messalianic pretensions. He insisted in his *Rules* on the fact that the monk is anyone of the faithful who wishes to be thoroughly Christian to the very end. He did not wish to hear monasticism spoken of as a state above another. An apothegm of Marcarius specifies that "a monk is called a monk because he converses day and night with God".[180] This is a grace offered all Christians.

In this wide sense Christian ascesis protects the spirit from any hold on the part of the world. It recommends *overcoming evil by the creation of the good*. Thus ascesis is never anything but a

[179] Eph. 6, 11.
[180] Paul Evergetinos, *Synagoge Rematon*, Const. 1861, I, p. 75, c. 2.

means, a strategy. Evagrius gave the counsel never to make a passion out of the ascetic means against the passions. "Do not turn
into a passion the antidote of the passions," [181] he said. He thus
foresaw the ascetic obscurantism that would consider itself an end;
this comes from an excessive concentration on sin and from a
mortification in which ends and means are identical. "Because many
who used to weep over their sins have forgotten the aim of tears,
they have been seized with madness and have been led astray." [182]
Man can create a morbid and fantastic atmosphere where he sees
everywhere only evil and sin and where he lives in the company of
demons and in the fear of hell. We must admit that a certain kind
of ascetic literature fosters such a state of mind, but there is an
abyss between the Gospel and such literature. In the Gospel it is
God who speaks; in mediocre texts it is a misguided man who discourses without ever having assimilated the spirit of the Gospel.
Christ was a perfect ascetic, but he lived among men and descended
into their hell in order to bring his light there. Then the good thief
in a moment of repentance sees opening before him the door to
the kingdom, and tax-gatherers and sinners may perhaps advance
beyond "the just ascetics" on the path of salvation.

The Gospel is messianic and explosive; its rejection of the world
is very particular to it, for it is never ascetic but eschatological. It
sets before us the exigency of the end, the balance sheet, the passage to the pleroma. During the liturgy, before the anaphora, there
is a command to close the doors of the church. In fact one closes
the doors of time and opens the one giving access to eternity; all
history enters and finds itself "in the nuptial chamber of Christ".[183]

The Gospel ascetic is a witness and an apostle. That is why the
monastic tradition, later than that of the desert, dwelt upon the
letters of St. John, and insisted on love of neighbor and the ascesis
of the heart. It is striking in its excess, not of fear, but of overflowing love and of cosmic tenderness "for every creature, even
for reptiles and demons".[184]

---

[181] *De Oratione*, 8.
[182] *Ibid.*
[183] St. Maximus the Confessor, *Mystagogie*, ch. 15.
[184] St. Isaac, Wensinck, *op. cit.*, p. 341.

The "individual salvationist" who is concerned only with the salvation of his soul manifests a dangerous distortion. We can never keep ourselves alone before God; we are saved only together, "collegially", as Solviev said: *he will be saved who saves others.* St. Dorotheus [185] gives a beautiful and clear picture of salvation under the form of a circle. Its center is God, and all men are on the circumference. In directing themselves toward God, each one follows a ray from the circle, and the nearer he approaches the center, the nearer the rays are to one another. Thus the shortest distance between God and man passes through the neighbor. Those exclusively devoted to action should understand that the hermits, by their incessant prayer, intervened actively in history. The efficacy of all human action is dependent on the intercession of their prayer, on the flame of their prayer that they send into the heart of the world. They know that man cannot respond to the entreaties of earth, and that is why they become hermits. St. Isaac the Syrian (in his *Sentences*) said so to his disciple: "Here, my brother, is a commandment that I give you—let mercy turn the balance of your scales until the moment that you feel in yourself the mercy that God feels toward the world." At this moment of maturity the recluse can return to the world.

This ascesis requires a great lucidity in order to see oneself as one really is. The balance that is sought is accompanied by a clear vision of one's own reality, but it advises against too much self-analysis. To look perpetually at oneself as in a mirror can cause a morbid state of excessive scruples. More than anywhere else perfect moderation is necessary here, as well as an experienced guide and the beneficial atmosphere of a living community.

Self-love and its tyrannic wishes build a wall between the soul and God; the art of obedience destroys it.

Origen admirably explains the ministry of the elders: "In every place where masters are found, Jesus Christ is in the midst of them, on condition, however, that the masters keep themselves in the temple and never leave it." [186] "The temple" for Origen meant an uninterrupted contemplation of Jesus.

[185] *Philocalie* (in Russian), II, 617.
[186] *Hom. in Luc.*, 20.

10
The Ascetic Effort

S piritual men always placed themselves in a concrete situation where efforts that were possible would open the soul and make it receptive and active. They were never concerned with doctrinal abstractions, with a search for merits or of a pharmaceutical mixture of grace and freedom. They left this preoccupation to theologians and expressed themselves only in terms of experience. "God *does everything* in us . . . What is ours is the good disposition of our will." [187] If they spoke of "labor and sweat", they meant the human action within the divine action. We can formulate it in this manner: it is God who "works", and it is man who "sweats".

Asceticism has nothing to do with moralism. The contrary of sin is not virtue but the faith of the saints. Moralism exercises natural forces, and its fundamental voluntarism submits human behavior to moral imperatives. We know how fragile and inefficacious is every autonomous and immanent ethical system, for it offers no vivifying source. We can respect a law, but we can never love it as we love a person—Jesus Christ, for example. Christ is not the principle of good but good incarnate. That is why in the tragic conflicts of existence, in the depths of some overwhelming sorrow or loneliness, moral and sociological principles are powerless. They do not have the power to say to a paralytic: "Get up and walk!" They cannot pardon or absolve, wipe out a fault or raise the dead. Erected into a system, their rigid appearance of being impersonal and general hides the pharisaism of "the pride of the humble". This is pride's most dangerous form, for once "pride is taken for humility, the malady is without remedy".[188]

On the other hand, the "virtue" of the ascetics has an entirely different resonance and designates the human dynamism set in motion by the presence of God. There is no question here of any

[187] St. Maximus the Confessor, *Ad. Thal.,* q. 54; *P.G.,* 90, 512D.
[188] Ignace Brianchaninov, *Oeuvres* (in Russian), Vol. I, p. 619.

"meritorious" work. "God is our creator and savior; he is not the one who measures and weighs the price of our works." [189]

No juridical idea of recompense is applicable here. "My child, give me your heart." These words of the Old Testament already announce the Gospel. "Seek the kingdom of God and all these things shall be given you besides."[190] In seeking the one thing necessary, man puts himself in harmony with it, and gives his heart as an offering. What comes from God is the kingdom, and this is a gratuitous gift. "If God regarded merits, then no one would enter into the kingdom of God."

Spiritual men in their search for salvation are not concerned with the mercantile calculations of those who are too interested in their own lot. Humility forbids us to feel ourselves "saved", but it makes us think ceaselessly of the salvation of others. The soul is occupied above all with the destiny of God in the world, and with the response that God expects from man. In the vision of mystics, God sometimes appears as abandoned and suffering in his wounded love. If it is necessary to save anything in this world, it is not man before all else, but the love of God, for he has first loved us and his power bears and sustains the expected response. In the interaction of grace and sin formulated by the theologians, spiritual men contemplate the interaction of the *two fiats,* the encounter of the descending love of God and the ascending love of man.

If "man is condemned and saved at the same time",[191] and if "the Church is the salvation of those who are perishing",[192] it can be a question only of the full expression of our faith. It is the free choice not of "works" but of the irresistible desire to be a child of God. It is for me to open the door of my soul so that he can enter in. I can only prostrate myself and hide my face as did the disciples on Thabor, blinded by the splendor of his presence. The violence of which the Gospel speaks has reference to the heart of man. That is why "God will judge the *hidden* secrets of men".[193] He will judge them because man is master of his heart.

[189] *Philocalie, P.G.,* 65, 929.
[190] Luke 12, 31.
[191] St. Ambrose, *P.L.* 15, 1502.
[192] St. Ephrem the Syrian, quoted by Father George Florovsky, *Les Pères du IVᵉ siècle* (Paris, 1931), p. 232, in Russian edition.
[193] Rom. 2, 16.

11
Progression of the Spiritual Life

S een from below, the spiritual life seems to be an incessant combat, an "invisible struggle", where every pause becomes a regression. Seen from above, it is the acquisition of the gifts of the
Holy Spirit. This double movement stands out clearly in the prayer
addressed to the Holy Spirit: "Purify us from all stain", but also
"Come and *dwell* within us."

This purification begins by a very realistic vision of one's state.
"Know thyself" was the ascetic teaching of Socrates. "No one can
know God unless he first knows himself." [194] "The one who has
seen his sin is greater than he who raises the dead." "He who has
seen himself is greater than he who has seen the angels." [195] A man's
vigorous penetration into the darkness of his heart of hearts, though
it is a formidable undertaking, gives him the power to judge himself. He must make the descent supplied with an ascetic scaphander,
the spirit of discernment, in order to explore its caverns peopled by
phantoms, and to seize in action his perverted will, and his anticipated death, in short, his irremediable natural deficiency. This is
the triple barrier of nature, sin and death that the Lord has passed
through for us all. The vision must be brief, instantaneous, in order
to avoid all pleasure in sorrow or despair. Sin is never a subject of
contemplation; we must rest our glance on what obliterates it—
grace. The soul can now truly utter the cry: "From the abyss of my
iniquity I invoke the abyss of your mercy."

The ascent is gradual. Thus *the heavenly ladder* of St. John
Climacus describes the upward progress in following the rungs or
steps in the order that he has studied perfectly. Charity, for example, is placed at the end, crowning the ascension and situated at

[194] *Philocalie* (in Russian), Vol. V, p. 159.
[195] St. Isaac, *Sentences.*

the top of the ladder. As a shrewd pedagogue, the saint warns against any activity of emotional love, for here it is a question of crucified love. The great spiritual men left their solitude and returned to the world at the moment of their perfect maturity. The wisdom of Climacus shows souls how to avoid many failures and disappointments, for some souls are too impatient, forgetting the words, "Physician, cure thyself." [196]

Mindful of the *metanoia* or conversion, the spiritual life takes for its point of departure *humility*. A spiritual man is a saint who confesses himself a sinner. "Anthony said in groaning: Who will then escape? And a voice answered him: Humility." [197] Abbot Sisoes at the moment of his death, being already fully enlightened, said humbly: "I have not even begun my penance." [198] These words mean that penance is the more and more acute consciousness of the love of God and of the inadequate response of man. It is not an act that can be finished, but a constant state of soul which deepens the nearer it approaches the end.

For the ascetic, humility means the art of finding his own place. "He who knows his exact measure possesses perfect humility." [199] If men of the world covet what is inordinate and excessive, and desire to be the master and the bridegroom, the Gospel gives us a luminous picture of humility. St. John the Baptist finds all his joy in being only the friend of the bridegroom, and the Blessed Virgin finds her joy in being the handmaid of the Lord. They diminish in order that the other, the true bridegroom and master, may increase. One is in function with the other. God does not take his exact place among men except when he finds a perfect conformity. He came "unto his own", and he was received by his friend and his handmaid. Their humility is an exact replica of the divine humility, of the kenosis of the servant of Yahweh, of "the man of sorrows". It reflects and follows a reversal of values; the pantocrator becomes the lover of men, and the king the crucified servant.

"Among those born of women there has not risen a greater

---

[196] Luke 4, 23.
[197] *P.G.*, 65, 77B.
[198] *P.G.*, 65, 396.
[199] Callistus and Ignatius, *Philocalie* (in Russian) Vol. V, p. 330.

than John the Baptist." [200] These words are antithetical for they abolish the limits of the covenants. To the "greater" corresponds the enigmatic. "Yet the least in the kingdom of heaven is greater than he." St. John is at the same time the greatest and the least, and he is the greatest *because he is the least*. Hearing the voice of the bridegroom, his friend says: "This my joy, therefore, is made full." [201] The joyous self-effacement is so deep that at this level the bridegroom and his friend converge in the ineffable grandeur that unites them. God had become man and man had become God to the point that people asked themselves whether John was not the Christ.[202] Now for all of us God manifestly places St. John and the virgin at the summit of the universal priesthood, as a "guiding image" in the service of his Church. This is clearly shown in the composition of the *Deisis,* the icon that represents the Lord in kingly garments with his mother on his right hand.[203]

Nietzsche commited a flagrant error in declaring that Christianity is the religion of slaves. Contrary to all plebian and vindictive resentment of offenses, the Christian confesses his guilt, and this is the attitude of a nobleman. No confusion is possible between humility and humiliation, weakness or spineless resignation. Humility is the greatest power, for it radically suppresses all spirit of resentment, and it alone can get the better of pride. The best definition of it would be to say that it *places the axis of a human being in God*.

From the psychiatric point of view, self-centeredness is indicative of every hysteric neurosis; it makes the universe turn around the human ego: "I, and no one else." The desire of equality caused the fall of Lucifer, notes St. Gregory Nazianzen. According to St. Gregory of Nyssa, Satan was offended at learning of the creation of man in the image of God. Likewise Islam shows him in revolt, refusing to bow down before Adam. The anti-Christ in Soloviev's *Legend* [204] becomes conscious of his demoniacal nature at the moment he feels the impossibility of prostrating and adoring any-

[200] Matt. 11, 11.
[201] John, 3, 29-30.
[202] Luke, 3, 15.
[203] See our work *La Femme et le Salut du Monde,* p. 224-230.
[204] In *Les trois entretiens.*

thing but his ego. We go back here to the source of the sin that explains the aim of ascesis: to break pride and to make humility the unshakable foundation of the human spirit: "To allow oneself to be ground between the grindstones of humility in order to become a sweet and agreeable bread for our Lord." [205]

The Golden Legend tells us the story of a humble man who had two "right hands". He had the habit of putting into his right hand all the joys received each day and all his sorrows into his left hand. It was his left hand that was always full. Then, through a spirit of humility, all that fell into his left hand, he put into his right hand, and his life became all light and joy.

[205] An ascetic adage that goes back to the words of St. Ignatius of Antioch, Rom. 4, 1.

12
The Passions and the Technique of Temptation

The biblical account of "the forbidden fruit" stresses the power of suggestion. It arouses desires by its aspect that is at the same time sensual and aesthetic. "The tree was good for food, pleasing to the eyes, and desirable." The arrow of temptation that wounded human freedom and perverted its choice went beyond the formal disobedience. We can see the essential of the fall: the desirable fruit, sensually coveted, immerses man in his life of the senses chosen in preference to a spiritual deepening of his communion with God. Man appears guilty not so much negatively by disobedience, but positively by not enriching himself by nearness to God. "If he had attached himself to God from the very first movement of his being, he would have immediately attained his perfection," says St. Gregory of Nyssa.[206]

Under the appearance of charms that attract, the fruit symbolizes a secret covetousness of the attributes of God. The love of the human heart, originally directed toward the being of God, is no longer centered on its object, but deviating, has oriented itself only to his attributes, the source of enjoyment. The grace of "resemblance" gives place to the magic of equality. "You will be as God."

The mystic image of a *fruit consumed* is not a chance one; it is clearly of a eucharistic nature. Evil, a principle initially exterior to innocent man, is introduced, by this consuming, within a human being. Evil thus becomes interior to man; on the other hand, it is God who has become exterior to him. The order is perverted; the biological animal seems foreign to the true nature of man, for the animal was assumed *before* its spiritualization, before man had arrived at the mastery of the spiritual over the material. Communion with nature, good in itself, proved to be bad since it was

[206] *P.G.*, 46, 373.

precocious. The error came from a premature identification. Clement of Alexandria sees original sin in the fact that "our ancestors gave themselves to procreation before the appointed time".[207]

Good in itself, animal nature, on account of the perversion of the hierarchy of values, now constitutes a permanent threat of causing the downfall of man. It was the axiological faculty of appreciation, the spirit of discernment, that was wounded. "Outside God, reason became like the beasts and the demons, and estranged from its nature, it desires what is foreign to it." [208] Illegitimate concupiscence is *against* nature, and then the human being is dominated by his passions, by the life of the senses. That is why the ascesis before all else neutralizes the passions in order to objectify and exteriorize these deifugal tendencies that withdraw man from God.

We can see this remedy at work in studying the sacrament of confession. "A hidden thought destroys the heart," remarks St. Cassian.[209] The action of evil can be traced to the redoubtable *philautia,* the self-love that encloses a man within himself. On the contrary, the opening up of the soul hinders the formation of complexes, denounces them and cures morbid scruples.[210] This is why confession entails the avowal of guilt, followed by absolution. For Clement of Alexandria, the confessor is like "an angel of penance", capable of penetrating and opening the souls of sinners; he is a "physician of God". "You have come to the doctor, do not return without being cured," says the prayer before confession. Likewise the Council of Trullo (692) defines that "those who have received from God the power of binding and loosening behave as physicians attentive to find the particular remedy that is required by each penitent and each fault of the penitent".[211]

An age-old experience clearly shows the danger of repressions and the liberating power of confession. "Many passions are hidden in our soul, but they escape our attention," says Evagrius.[212] This is

---

207 *Strom.* III, 18.
208 St. Gregory of Palamas, *Homilia,* 51.
209 *P.L.,* 49, 162.
210 Dorotheus, *P.G.,* 88, 1640C.
211 Canon 102.
212 *Centuries,* VI, 52.

because the fault is rooted in the soul and poisons man's whole interior. It calls for a surgical operation that will cut the roots and exteriorize the fault. This necessitates the presence of a witness who will listen, and by thus destroying the solitude, will bring the penitent into the communion of the body. Psychoanalysis has re-discovered the value of confession. It tries in its own way to lead the patient to accept a dialogue, to go beyond his very inaptitude to dialogue and his anguish that hinders him from going toward others.

Sozomen (5th century) declares forcefully: "To ask pardon one must necessarily confess his sins." [213] The soul is unburdened of the sin, but how can this sin be made non-existent? A bad con-science comes not only from remorse for the fault commited but also from a nostalgia for lost innocence. Man seeks pardon, but in the utmost depths of his heart he craves for the annihilation of the evil; for this desired abolition, sacramental absolution is required. The fault has been exteriorized, even recounted and thus made objective, projected, so to speak, to the outside; yet it can plague him from the exterior. Sacramental absolution alone can destroy it and bring a total cure. Psychiatrists who are believers know the liberation accomplished by the action of the sacrament, and they often complete their treatment by sending their patients to an "ecclesial clinic". The immense importance of confession is in this final liberation. For a man to become free again, he must know how to utilize his past, even if it has been a guilty one, in order to create a present that is more innocent. He must transcend the passive receptivity of his soul and its behavior, subject to automatic causes, and go toward the creations of his spirit that has become again unsullied after absolution. To escape henceforth from these causes means that he has become master of his destiny, leaving himself open to the liberating action of the divine forces.

The act of pardon places us in the heart of the relationship between God who is holy and man who is the sinner, and we must grasp the infinite gravity of this act. It is not the almighty power of God to efface and to make non-existent that is involved here; it is a question of Christ, who, according to St. Paul, canceled "the

[213] *P.G.*, 67, 1460.

decree against us . . . nailing it to the cross".[214] If "the lamb is immolated from the foundation of the world", this means that the creation of the world was already rooted in the immolation of the creator, and that is why the power to pardon comes from the price of the blood shed by the crucified lamb. This is because Christ takes *on himself* all the transgressions and all the crimes of the world, and for this remains in agony until its end. Because he thus responds to the love of his Father by his ineffable love *in our stead,* he has the moral power to efface and pardon and to make us innocent children of the Father. The Lord's Prayer, "Forgive us our trespasses as we forgive", conditions the pardon of ourselves by an "imitation" of God on our part; we are invited to descend, in Christ's footsteps, to the hell of universal guilt where all are culpable. Every faithful member of the Orthodox Church confesses before communion: "Of all sinners, I am the first."

The prayer before confession, accompanied by the reading of Psalm 50, has an immense significance; it testifies to the reattachment, the preliminary reunion of the sinner with the Church. Through the prayers of the priest, the penitent is taken in charge, as it were, by the Church. It is by her that he is brought and presented before the face of God. It is in finding himself in the maternal bosom of the Church that a man can truly confess his sins and receive the cure, for each sin exteriorizes man in regard to the body of Christ. Reintegrated into the Church, man can weep the tears of repentance. These tears, says Symeon the New Theologian, "purify and confer the second baptism of which the Lord speaks, the rebirth in water and in the Spirit; the baptism of tears is no longer a figure of the truth, it is truth itself".[215] Every automatic effect of the sacrament is excluded; the rebirth by the Spirit requires full consciousness on the part of the one who crosses the abysses "in shuddering".

The ascesis of the spiritual life follows the road traced out by repentance and penance. It aspires above all to free man from the ascendancy of his passions. In order to attain this end, it fosters spiritual attention, a guard over the heart. "I sleep but my heart

214 Col. 2, 14.
215 *Chap. theolog., gnostiques et pratiques,* I, ch. 35-36.

watches." Even in a state of sleep it is watchful. Vigilance thus practiced permits a man to recognize evil before being tempted to commit it.

The ascetics give a minute description of the progression of evil, laying bare the technique or the mechanism, on the whole rather simplistic, of temptation.

The first movement of "contamination" comes from a representation, image, idea, desire crossing our mind; something very fleeting that arises abruptly and solicits our attention. From the subconscious the appeal rises to consciousness and makes an effort to be kept there. This is not yet sin, far from it, but it is the presence of a suggestion. It is in this first moment that the immediate reaction of the attention on the watch is decisive. The temptation is going to go away or it is going to remain. Spiritual writers make use of an image that was familiar in the desert: "Strike the serpent on the head" before he enters the cell. If the whole serpent enters, the struggle will be much more laborious.

If the attention does not react, the following phase passes to pleasure. A willing attention to the tempting solicitation causes a certain pleasure, becoming an equivocal attitude that is already cooperating. St. Ephrem speaks of the "pleasant conversation" of the soul with a persistent suggestion.

An enjoyment by anticipation, imaginary at the moment, marks the third stage. A tacit agreement, an unavowed consent, orients one toward an accomplishment judged possible, for it is passionately desirable. In principle, the decision has indeed been taken; in the effective coveting of the object, the sin has been committed mentally. This is the judgment of the Gospel on the impure look in which adultery has already been pre-consummated.

The fourth stage effectively consummates the act. It forms the beginning of a passion, of a thirst henceforth unquenchable. When it has become a habit, the passion neutralizes every resistance. The person disintegrates in the avowal of his powerlessness; he is bewitched and tends toward his implacable end: despair, the fearful *acedia,* disgust or anxiety of heart, madness or suicide, in all cases, spiritual death.

III

THE CHARISMS OF THE
SPIRITUAL LIFE
AND THE
MYSTIC ASCENSION

1
Evolution of the Spiritual Life in the East and in the West

In the West, after the contributions of the Irish missionaries, who introduced a most austere rule—St. Columban's *maxima pars regulae monachorum mortificatio est*—St. Benedict's spirituality dominated. It followed the ancient tradition of St. Basil, above all, and of St. Cassian. A very well-balanced ascesis regulated and divided the monk's time among the *lectio divina,* chanting of the office, fasting and manual labor. However, this balance did not last long. Cluny made the offices more solemn, prolonged them too, in order to lessen the manual work that was not very attractive to the monks. Citeaux was established in reaction to Cluny; it returned to the greatest severity in the rule, and was striking in the sobriety and bareness of its style of life, and by the deliberate poverty of its abbeys: *cum Christe paupere paupers.*

The Camaldolesi of St. Romuald and the Carthusians of St. Bruno cultivated the state of hermits and recluses at the side of the cenobites. From the beginning of the Middle Ages, penance was introduced among the austere hermits with the extreme means of discipline, flagellation and the hairshirt. It was reminiscent of, dangerous perhaps, the ascesis of the desert, to which was added a completely new element—mortification practiced in view of an expiation for sins committed and also in view of a reparation for the sins of the world. It is sufficient here to name Peter Damian.

The 11th century saw the rise of the very popular devotion of pilgrimages to sanctuaries—Jerusalem, St. James of Compostella, Rome. A mass of pilgrims took to the road as beggars along all the routes. The Crusades led the Westerners to Palestine. This discovery was decisive for Western mysticism; it made a strong impression on the imagination of the West and aroused an ardent imitation, a conformation to the humanity of the historic Christ of the Gospel.

The 12th century turned its ascesis and spirituality toward the image of Jesus poor, humiliated and crucified. St. Francis espoused Lady Poverty and received the stigmata. Later Henry Suso gave himself to extreme mortification in imitation of Jesus scourged.

In the 13th century the Dominicans stressed study and made an ascesis of it. On the other hand, St. Bernard and St. Bonaventure accentuated the monastic vows and again took up the classical stages of the spirituality of St. Denys: *purgatio, illuminatio, perfectio*.

The end of the Middle Ages shows a certain lack of spirit and an impoverishment of the spiritual life. Scholastic studies were directed to the intellect and replaced the *lectio divina* and prayerful contemplation; prayer itself became formalistic. What is called *devotio moderna* widened the distance between spirituality and a more and more speculative theology. The Dutch school of Gerard Groote inspired Thomas à Kempis whose *Imitation of Christ* summarizes the tendencies of the recent past and makes concrete this unfortunate divorce. Union with God was accompanied by a certain anti-intellectualism, a reaction against the theology of the schools and knowledge. The 15th century, in its effort to escape the dryness and rigidity of formal rules, threw itself into the emotionalism of sorrow and suffering. Intense devotion to the suffering humanity of Christ developed into a cult of dolorism with forms of mortification that are really disquieting.

The Renaissance humanized ascesis, aligning it with its integral but still devout humanism. Spirituality broke up into a multitude of devotional practices. In the 16th century, Ignatian spirituality made ascesis a method and a technique of conversion, and St. Francis de Sales formed, in the beginning of the following century, a psychological ascesis of the interior states. They both went beyond the monastic environment and began a secular ascesis.

Ascesis became more psychological in paying attention to the states of consciousness. St. Thomas had already analyzed the ecstasy of St. Paul and had shown a lively interest in the relation between soul and body and in the modes of knowledge. Likewise, with St. Teresa and St. John of the Cross, Spanish mysticism analyzed the interior and psychological aspect of the mystic ascent.

The ascesis of St. Cyran, Port Royal and Jansenism mistrusted human nature. Its soteriological and pastoral preoccupation accentuated the rigorist austerity of the penitential practices imposed upon the faithful. Besides its moral relaxation, the 18th century, in which the austerity of the 17th was in a sense prolonged, manifested a spirituality that appears intellectually impoverished and somewhat static, without the spontaneity and warmth of former times.

A very special reaction manifested itself in quietism, but it was with St. Margaret Mary Alacoque that the entirely new devotion to the Sacred Heart showed *reparational ascesis*. Mortification in order to satisfy divine justice and on behalf of all sinners took the place of the effort for personal perfection.

The shock of the French Revolution accentuated the practices of reparational penances and expiatory ascesis. The psychologism and rationalism of the 19th century still more completely separated spirituality from dogma and theology. At present we are witnessing a vigorous return to sources in the patristic past and original monasticism.

If we turn toward the East, we shall see that it has remained faithful to the spirituality of former times that was common to both East and West. Eastern monasticism had already been perfected in the 5th and 6th centuries. Under Justinian it was proclaimed "a sacred thing" and "a mystery", because it expresses in a compact and exemplary form the universal vocation of the priesthood of the faithful, because each and everyone is called to interiorize and adapt it. The priesthood does not enter here except as a sacramental aid; it does not constitute a necessary element.

As an organic part of the Church, monastic spirituality synthesizes the religious ideal of a life proposed in its general outlines to all men. The dogmatic definitions on hesychasm in the 14th century only stated precisely what had existed from the beginning and showed the homogeneous character of Eastern spirituality. It is inseparable from "mystic theology", the theology of the mystery that had been completely formed during the golden age of the Fathers.

At the present time, the two spiritualities—Eastern and Western —complement each other; we can apply the saying of Evagrius: "The *gnosticos* (knower) and the *practicos* (doer) have met, and in the middle of the two stood the Lord." [1] They met in a search for the essence of the experience of the past in order to establish a balanced spirituality, freed from the extreme forms that were stressed too much in the ascesis of a past age, a spirituality that has its axis in eschatology, fully conscious of the present state of the world, and preoccupied, above all, with its destiny.

[1] *Aux moines qui habitent dans les coenobia,* 121.

2
Passage from the Old Testament to the New

In the days of the old covenant, spiritual life was manifested in three forms—almsgiving, prayer and fasting. It received its completion in the Sermon on the Mount that placed it in the service of evangelical charity. The post-apostolic age added to it martyrdom and celibacy without making them a novelty. Indeed in late Judaism, believers sealed the confession of their faith with their blood, and, on the other hand, St. John the Baptist reflected the spirituality of the Essenes, and the Lord and the apostles scandalized no one by their celibacy. On the whole, this spirituality responded to the call of the one thing necessary and sought freedom from the bonds of this world in order to go more joyfully to meet the one who was coming.

The great joy of the first spiritual teachers, their optimism also, came from their unshakable confidence in the image of God. This conformity of the divine and the human, already full of grace by its nature, Christ manifests and renders efficacious for all. In its dynamic function, it is "a guiding image" toward the fullness of a cure. The Bible forcefully stresses the therapeutic idea of salvation, and thus conditions Christian spirituality at its very source.

In the light of revelation, salvation has nothing juridical about it; it is not the sentence of a tribunal. The verb *yacha* in Hebrew means "to be without restraint", at ease. In a wider sense, it means to deliver, to save from a danger, from an illness, from death; this makes clear the very particular meaning of reestablishing a vital balance, of *curing*. The substantive *yéchà*, salvation, signifies total deliverance with peace—*schalom*—at the end. In the New Testament *sōtēria* in Greek comes from the verb *sōdzō;* the adjective *sōs* corresponds to the Latin *sanus* and means to restore health to

157

one who has lost it, to save from death, the natural end of every illness. That is why the expression "Thy faith has *saved* thee" includes the version "thy faith has *cured* thee", the two terms referring to the same act of divine pardon, an act that touches soul and body in their very unity. In accordance with this idea, the sacrament of penance is thought of as a "medical clinic", and St. Ignatius of Antioch calls the eucharist, *pharmakson,* a remedy of immortality.

Jesus thus appears as the divine healer, saying: "It is not the healthy who need a physician, but they who are sick . . . I have come to call sinners, not the just." [2] Sinners are the sick who are threatened with spiritual death, more fearful than that of the body. We can then specify the therapeutic meaning of salvation: it is the cure of a being and the elimination of the germ of mortality. This is why the Savior called himself the life, and the saved receive eternal life. The end joins the beginning when man, having received the breath of life, lives by participation in the Holy Spirit, creator of life. Ascesis seeks to refind that deep and adequate conformity of man to his own truth, his norm, as the fertility of the earth and the beauty of a woman are conformed to theirs. Ascesis is practiced in order to render man very much like God's thought of him. In this perspective, "the works of faith" are neither means nor "merits", but symptoms of health-salvation.

The extent of evil can be measured by the power of its antidote. The sick are cured by a treatment that befits the stature of God. The physician, instead of the patient, passes through death and inaugurates his universal remedy: "Unless the grain of wheat falls into the ground and dies, it remains alone. But if it dies, it brings forth much fruit." [3] The cross is planted at the threshold of the new life—*vita nova*—and the water of baptism receives the sacramental value of the blood of Christ. From then on, ascesis teaches participation in the "health" of the Savior, but this entails a victory over death and therefore a preliminary purification. Only the trial of suffering can so deepen and purify life as to lead to conscious and true joy. The Church announces that "by the cross joy has come to all of us", and this message traces for us an unchanging and perfect

[2] Matt. 9, 2-13.
[3] John 12, 24.

itinerary. If every destiny is thus placed under the sign of "the carrying of the cross", "the cross is vivifying" and its joy transcends all enjoyment of dolorism and agonizing sensibility. Ascesis leads beyond psychism, and spiritual mastery fosters extreme sobriety of feeling.

The Old Testament expectation of the messianic age had already formed a pilgrim type. The New Testament fulfillment only accentuated more forcefully this state of *homo viator;* it entrusted him with a precise and human task.

According to the Gospel, time is short; this world as we see it is passing away; now that the bridegroom has been taken away, we can no longer enjoy the world and live in the penultimate values of existence. Qualitatively, since pentecost, we live in the latter times. This situation suggests a great liberation from the cares of the world in order to make our awaiting active. Such an ascetic "activism" corresponds to the taste of our age, which in its spirit of invention and its social preoccupations is opposed to quietism. If we see that spiritual men constantly insist on manual work, this is not simply to occupy their leisure time, because ascetics earn their living in order to practice charity.[4] The true "impassibility", according to Evagrius, "is accompanied by an immense love of God and a boundless fervor for the works of charity".[5] An angel revealed to Pachomius that "the will of God is that we should put ourselves in the service of men". Pachomius later said that "the love of God consists in our taking trouble one for another".[6] Thus ascetics were true to man's task, discovering in it the dimension of the kingdom; they saw perfection in the fear "of wounding love, however slightly".[7]

The Fathers were completely conscious of the changing forms of ascesis. The *Apothegms* recounts this incident. "The holy fathers were prophesying on the last days. 'What have we ourselves done?' they wondered. One of them, the great Abbot Ischyrion, answered: 'We have observed the commandments of God.' 'And those who will follow us,' continued the others, 'what will they do?' Ischyrion re-

---

4 See St. Basil, *Greater Rule,* 37.
5 *Pract.* II, 57.
6 *Vie copte de saint Pacôme.*
7 Cassian, *Conf.* IX.

plied: 'Those will succeed in doing only half of what we have done.' The fathers still insisted. 'How will it be with those who come after them?' 'The men of that age,' the abbot answered, 'will not be rich in works; the time of the great temptation will arise against them; those then who are good will be greater than we are and than our fathers were.' " [8]

Today the spectacular practices of former times have become interior. Exploits are hidden under the mantle of daily life. The superhuman has become more human; it takes the exact measure of the modern world, of its needs and its mentality. Spirituality, without compromising anything, seeks to adapt itself to the evolution of the human psyche. Thus ascesis in its beginnings manifested a biological exuberance; now nervousness and lack of resistance of the normal constitution would advise rather the avoidance of every apparent violence. Medicine, where it can, suppresses suffering and thus makes man more vulnerable, more sensitive to physical pain by the fact that pain has become rarer.

Ascesis places its emphasis elsewhere, and very fortunately it shares the major preoccupations of all free philosophic reflections. After Jung, psychologists know well that a little freedom causes anguish, but much freedom cures it. This is exactly the aim of ascesis: to transcend every limit, to expand souls by the greatest daring of love, and to develop the person by means of gifts and charisms.

[8] *Apophtegmata Patrum, P.G.,* 65, 241. See Dom Stolz, *L'Ascèse chrétienne,* p. 8.

3
Charisms of the Spiritual Life

1. *The Spirit of Discernment, Impassibility, Silence, Vigilance, Repentance and Humility.*

St. John Climacus describes the spiritual life under the reassuring figure of *scala paradisi*. The heavenly powers aid human efforts. The angels who go up and down "Jacob's ladder" accompany man on this journey in which he receives charisms. St. Cyril of Jerusalem enumerates some of them: "For one, the Spirit strengthens his temperance, to another he teaches what concerns mercy, to still another how to fast, and in short, to practice the exercises of the spiritual life." [9]

The import of these words is that the spiritual life is entirely and at once charismatic. Above all, *the spirit of discernment* shows how not to confuse the end with the means. Evagrius shrewdly notes that the worst error would be to make a passion out of the struggle against passion. "Prayer, fasting, vigils, and every other practice . . . are only indispensable means to attain the acquisition of the Holy Spirit," teaches St. Seraphin.[10] Here the end is stated very precisely. St. Isaac adds that the simplicity of God unites but the complexity of evil disperses.[11]

The Sixth Ecumenical Council noted this dispersion and affirmed that "sin is the sickness of the soul"; it directed its attention to a therapeutic ascesis.

That is why St. Paul,[12] in praying very particularly for the spirit

[9] *Cath. myst.,* 16, 12.
[10] *Entretien sur le but de la vie chrétienne.*
[11] Wensinck, *op. cit.,* p. 202.
[12] Phil. 1, 10.

161

of discernment, had in mind the axiological function of appreciation, a spiritual prophylactic that renders a man capable of distinguishing and of making decisive choices. Here an obstacle arises: every conscious command arouses a secret resistance from the subconscious and this paralyzes the will. St. Paul remarks: "For I do not understand what I do . . . For I do not the good that I wish, but the evil that I do not wish, that I perform." He discovered the interior law that fights against the law of understanding; he thus formulated the law of irrational resistance that comes from the subconscious.[13]

The Bible knows well the impenetrable lower depths of the human being. "More tortuous than all else is the human heart, beyond remedy; who can understand it? I, the Lord, alone can probe the mind and test the heart," [14] which means the human ego and the obscure sphere that surrounds it. The Gospel judges a man by the contents of his heart, by the object of his desires, by his Eros. "It is from the heart that man draws good things and bad." The possibilities are in one direction or the other.

The great masters of ascesis were perfectly clear on the role of the subconscious. Evagrius teaches: "Many passions are hidden in our soul, but escape our attention. It is temptation which, coming suddenly, reveals them." [15]

"Depth psychology" very fortunately comes to give scientific substance to ascetic art and to aid man to understand himself. It analyzes the dynamism of affectivity, the obscure zone of the unconscious, the irrational root of the soul where the instinct of "the will to live" is active. Jarred by the real, subject to a social censure, this interior world is remodeled; a part of its vitality is repressed; reflexes of inhibition and compensation are elaborated. A mysterious and hidden life flows on beneath the threshold of consciousness, ceaselessly exercising its pressure. The person's health depends on the balance between the conscious and the subcon-

---

[13] Rom. 7, 15-23.

[14] Jer. 17, 9-10.

[15] *Centuries*, VI, 52. See Jung, *Types psychologiques*, p. 111. Jung quotes Cynesius, Bishop of Ptolemais, for whom the imagination is the middle sphere between the eternal and the temporal; it is through it that we live more fully.

scious, on the mind's capacity to project its light there, on integration with its "shadow".

Obscure and malevolent powers utilize man's psychic elements. In this sense Jung mentions a resemblance between complexes and demons. Ascetics counsel exercising the attention and discerning in the interior chaos of a soul the nature of the elements at work—animal, rational, or affective—and likewise they advise distinguishing between an interior or exterior cause, whether it is simply biological or more complex and moral. Thus Evagrius (in his *Antirrheticos*) specifies the somatic cause of gluttony and of lust, representing as they do perversion of the instincts to live and to survive. For St. Gregory Palamas, the passions coming from nature are less grave, and express only the weight of matter due to a failure to spiritualize it. In the 14th century, long before Freud, he spoke of sexual manifestations among very small children as *natural manifestations*. Sin and passions that are dangerous come from the mind.

The perverted will turns away from the original direction of the heart in order to seek the absolute in idols (the capital vices or passions that have been hypostasized); it throws itself into the cult of the ego with its self-love and its will to power, making of it an infernal self-idol. The transvaluation of values (*Umwertung*), the method practiced by the Viennese school, is used to unmask these idols in order to make the true absolute evident.

Psychology is in harmony with ascesis; it observes that too detailed memories of the past, too long a time of thinking about them, risks doing more harm than good. The Freudian method of introspection and of reducing the present to the past alienates man. It has been completed and surpassed by the Jungian method of prospection that leads to the construction of the future. Jung teaches the forging ahead that is formulated in the words of St. Paul: "Forgetting what is behind, I strain forward to what is before, I press on toward the goal." [16]

What is important are the present inclinations that permit a man to take cognizance and true measure of himself. Vigilance of mind, a guard over the heart, the invocation of the name of Jesus, are the

[16] Phil. 3, 13-14.

charisms that restrain and stop all interior colloquies with an evil suggestion before it becomes a tacit consent, or a passion that makes the soul captive. We must descend to the irrational roots of the soul, toward the clear or cloudy source in the imagination, and surprise its exact nature.

Psychoanalysis and ascesis have indeed understood this, and they search into the twisting ways in order to bring to them the light of the mind. This is because one cannot act on the subconscious by commands, for it is opposed to every direct order. One enters there most efficaciously by the imagination; one then discovers the great power of images.[17]

Indeed, in the face of the natural powerlessness of man to fulfill the Old Testament law and to submit to the prohibitions of the decalogue, the New Testament offers the grace of the beatitudes; even more, in order to arouse and sustain man's acts, grace operates by positive suggestions under the form of invitations and appeals. These suggestions are reinforced by "beautiful images", by the "absolute desirability" of the New Jerusalem that unfolds before our eyes in the grandiose description in the Apocalypse.

It is before all else the reconstruction of the *imago Dei,* of its initial form, tending toward God, as a copy toward its original. We can see the importance of the biblical notion of "image". By its nature of being an image, this structural form can be seized by the imagination, and consequently, only the imagination can penetrate subconscious and structure it in "the image of God".

The imagination always tends toward the incarnation of its images. To the suggestive power of art can be added the living language of symbols of sacred art. According to Jung: "Only the religious symbol sublimates totally." We say, "the symbol of faith", since the *Credo,* said liturgically, leads us beyond images and even symbols; it brings us into the presence of the persons invoked, there where the relations between the human *I* and the divine *thou* are made concrete. If Kant's categorical imperative is power-less, since it is abstract and impersonal, the Gospel, on the

---

[17] Ascesis purifies the imagination and then directs it toward what is be-yond the image. Such is the ultimate meaning of the Orthodox icon; it raises our spiritual gaze toward its own apophatic limit.

contrary, reveals the living person of Christ, the source of charismatic imperatives.

Origen had commented on the words of St. Paul, "until Christ is formed in you",[18] seeing in them the act of "imagining" Christ in the hearts of his disciples. The German word *ein-bilden* is very expressive here and designates the essence of the activity. Once his image is formed in the soul, the person of Christ in return forms the soul and transforms it into his own type: "It is no longer I that live, but Christ who lives in me." In the end the soul appears really Christified.

Ascesis thus constitutes an immense project of sublimation.[19] However, we must understand this in the sense of a tension toward *sublimissimum,* toward the Most High. It refines the imagination and practices fast of the eyes and spiritual hearing. Man ceaselessly collects innumerable images that surround him and invade him from within. He constantly undergoes suggestions coming from speeches, scientific formulas, political slogans, artistic forms,[20] human faces and cosmic landscapes. If everything in existence concurs in *suggesting,* in exercising a pressure on the soul, in impressing it, the "theodidacts",[21] those "taught by God", receive the strongest suggestion, for it is God who suggests by the creative images of his wisdom. Here the attention of the mind is required; Abbot Philemon tells us: "By your imagination look within your heart," for "the pure heart sees God as in a mirror".[22]

The purification of the heart comes above all from the liturgy where rite, dogma and art are closely bound together. Its images are symbols that lift our gaze to the level of the invisible presence of divinity. According to St. John Damascene, the icon is not a representation of the visible, but an apocalypse, a revelation of the hidden. Its power is maximal by reason of its opening upon the transcendental that has no image. The gaze thus purified and rendered watchful can now descend and scrutinize the interior of the soul and manifest it. "He who manifests his thoughts is soon

18 Gal. 4, 19.
19 See Kristian Schjelderup, *Die Askese* (Berlin, 1928).
20 See Baudouin, *Psychanalyse de l'Art.*
21 St. Macarius, *Hom.,* XV, 20.
22 *Philocalie* (in Russian), vol. III, p. 372.

cured; he who hides them makes himself sick." "It is an evident sign that a thought is from the demon when we blush to disclose it to our brother." [23]

John of Lycopolis expresses the tradition in ceaselessly returning to the need for watchful attention. "Judge your thoughts piously before God; if you cannot do this, ask one who is capable of discerning them." [24]

Such openness of soul and charismatic attention to what takes place within hinder the formation of complexes; wounds that are detected or declared do not grow worse.

Exterior behavior is always symptomatic of the inward state, and their intimate correspondence conditions and justifies corporal ascesis; but this relationship limits ascetic restraint to what is strictly necessary as an instrument to ward off enervating comfort and the tyranny of habits. The ideal state has the very paradoxical name of *apatheia* which means "impassible passion", and designates a very *impassioned* state, for it is a question of awakening the spirit from its sluggishness and making man wide awake, *neptikos*. It needs a whole life to live what faith affirms once for all, and it is for this reason that the spirit is watchful. St. Teresa of Avila said energetically that we should "neither creep, nor advance like a frog, nor walk with chicken steps". "What must one be? One must be a fire," notes St. Exupéry.[25]

Ascetic impassibility then is not insensibility. Neither does it seek to resemble those whom Bernanos called "the stoics with dry eyes", nor to cultivate delight in bloody mortifications and in the groanings of the flesh. By lack or by excess, the two destroy the balance, and manifest an ascesis that is illusory and "without fruit".[26] With ascetics, the capacity to become impassioned indicates their inward dynamism, which must be oriented, not suppressed. It receives its value from the goal to be attained, and this suppresses art for art, science for science, and above all, ascesis for ascesis. "The perfect soul is one whose passions are turned

---

[23] Cassian, *P.L.* 49, 161-162.
[24] See *Revue des Sciences religieuses,* 41 (1953), p. 526.
[25] *Pilote de Guerre* (Ed. Pléiade), p. 366.
[26] St. Macarius, *P.G.,* 34, 761; St. Dorotheus, *P.G.,* 88, 1780.

toward God," whose energies are directed toward divine love of men. This is why Diadochus says: "Woe to the knowledge that does not turn to loving." The state of the passions is centered on the one passion *par excellence,* evangelical charity, "ontological tenderness" toward every creature of God; this is the fundamental charism. "What is a charitable heart?" asks St. Isaac the Syrian. "It is a heart inflamed with charity for the entire creation, for men, birds, beasts, evil spirits, all creatures . . . moved by an infinite pity that is awakened in the hearts of those who are like to God." [27] Such a passionate lover "does not condemn either sinners or the children of this world . . . He desires to love and venerate all without any distinction", for "after God he esteems all men as God himself".[28] St. Symeon, following St. Paul, certainly speaks of himself when he confesses: "I know a man who would desire the salvation of his brothers with such ardor . . . that he would not even wish to enter the kingdom of heaven if in so doing he would have to separate himself from them." [29]

On a certain level, oral prayer gives place to contemplative prayer, in which the heart opens itself *in silence* before God. "When the Spirit comes, we must cease praying," St. Seraphin teaches. It is "the silence of the spirit" (hesychasm). The more alert the soul is, the more peaceful it is. In the counsel given by St. Seraphin to seek above all interior peace, the latter designates the hesychasm in which man becomes the *place* of God. If "the Word came forth from the Father in silence",[30] silence teaches men to give up their thoughtless chatter, and then the silent man becomes "a source of grace to the one who listens to him".[31]

The current opposition between adherence to the world and leaving the world is spatial. The basis of the problem is in the vertical dimension. "When you pray, enter into thy chamber and close the door." It is not a question of the place, but of a closed door. In this way El Greco used to seek colors in the depths of his

---

[27] Wensinck, *op. cit.,* p. 341.
[28] St. Nil, *P.G.,* 79, 1192C.
[29] *P.G.,* 120, 423.
[30] St. Ignatius of Antioch, Rom. 2, 1; *Magn.* 8, 2.
[31] St. Basil, *Lesser Rule,* CCVIII.

soul, and looking for inspiration, he used to draw all the curtains
of his studio and of his soul. We must know how to make a place
for silence, for recollection; without these moments, charged with
interior dynamism, the spiritual life risks being dissolved in sterile
agitation. When we attain to a certain maturity, the prayer of Jesus
teaches us to have these moments, even in public places, and to be
efficacious for others by our silence.

In these pauses of recollection, the masters of the spiritual life
strongly counsel against the states of ecstasy that belong only to
inexperienced beginners. In his progress, a man ought to aspire to
constant awareness of the invisible presence of God and to turn
aside relentlessly from every visual or sense phenomenon, all
curiosity, all seeking for "the mysterious". Evagrius strenuously
insists on this: "Do not strive during prayer to discern any image
or figure . . . otherwise you risk falling into madness." [32] Gregory
the Sinaite (15th century) advises: "Be watchful, friend of God.
If you see a light, or some image, or an angel, refuse to accept it . . .
When it seems to your spirit that you are drawn to the heights by
an invisible force, do not allow this and force yourself to work." [33]
As long as one can resist or oppose an apparition, it is a sign that
the phenomenon does not come from God. What comes from God
comes in an irresistible way. All the teachers strongly insist on the
extreme sobriety of what is spiritual and its lack of any material-
ization.

"If you see a young novice mounting by his own will to heaven,
seize him by the feet and throw him on the ground, because his
action would be of no value to him." [34] Satan disguised as an angel
of light came one day to a hermit to assure him of his spiritual
progress. The hermit contented himself with saying, not without
humor: "You must be making a mistake, it is to another person
that you have been sent; I have not made any spiritual progress." [35]

Unusual phenomena may disturb novices, but they have no connection with the spiritual life. The latter is always oriented toward
the interior. "If you are pure, heaven is within you, and it is within

[32] *De Oratione,* 114-116.
[33] *De la vie contemplative,* 10.
[34] *Vitae Patrum; P.L.,* 73, 932B-C.
[35] *P.L.,* 73, 965C.

you that you will see light, the angels, and the Lord of the angels." [36]

This entrance of the soul into itself is opposed, however, to any passive quietism. St. John Climacus insists on the dynamism of the spirit: "The one who keeps his fervor to the end does not cease to add, even to the end of his life, fire to fire, ardor to ardor, zeal to zeal, desire to desire." [37] "The Lord triumphs always, when he fights with Christian athletes. But if these are overcome, it is clear that they have deprived themselves of God by their unreasonable will." [38] The dynamism of the will is indeed required, for "God does nothing by himself alone", St. Macarius declares.[39] To a monk who had asked Anthony to pray for him, the abbot answered: "Neither shall I have pity on you, nor will God, if you do not put yourself seriously and particularly to prayer." [40]

The spiritual life then has nothing unconscious or passive about it. The soul's attention develops sensitivity to signs and warnings. A sluggish spirit lets these constant appeals pass by. Vigilance, on the contrary, fosters *repentance* which is an active manner of listening ceaselessly to the words: "Be perfect as your heavenly Father is perfect."

The giving up of repentance marks the cessation of the spiritual life and is accompanied by the fearful state called "the insensibility of a petrified heart". We must distinguish this from the "withdrawal of God" or "desolation", which the divine Teacher uses to teach the soul to be more humble. This dereliction is medicinal, notes Origen, and St. Macarius says: "Grace is taken away in order that we may seek it more." [41] Is not the sphere of the trial the very field of freedom? Once when St. Anthony had overcome his distress, he asked: "Where wert thou, Lord, during this time?" He received the answer: "Nearer than ever to thee." [42]

"We shall not be accused," says St. John Climacus, "of not

---

[36] St. Macarius, *P.G.*, 34, 776.
[37] *P.G.*, 88, 634C.
[38] St. Isaac, Wensinck, *op. cit.*, p. 340, p. 187.
[39] *P.G.*, 34, 757A.
[40] *P.G.*, 65, 80C.
[41] *Hom.* 27; *P.G.*, 34, 701D.
[42] *Apophtegmata Patrum.*

having performed miracles . . . but we shall surely have to answer
to God for not having wept ceaselessly for our sins." [43] Repentance
meditates constantly on man's refusal of crucified love. It is a
question here of tears, not of the soul but of the spirit. They are
considered a charismatic gift; they mingle with the tears of joy
and continue the purifying waters of baptism. "Blessed are they
who weep for they will be comforted." Such a repentance, according to St. John Damascene, is "the return to God from captivity",[44] and also "the salutary trembling fear before the door of the
kingdom".[45]

Evidently repentance is a form of humility. The two are not all
"virtues" but a permanent state of the soul. Only their power can
cure egocentric idolatry, self-love, pretensions, or inferiority complexes. Humility teaches "to be as if one were not", and "not to
know what one is". "To bow down before the divine majesty is
the highest victory," St. Bernard remarks profoundly.[46] The love of
God excludes all self-complacency. When St. Anthony asked to
be shown a model of piety, an angel led him to a very humble man.
In his prayer, this man used to present before God all men, thinking that there existed no one who was as great a sinner as himself.
Abbot Sisoes on his deathbed, already fully enlightened and surrounded by angels, sighed: "I have not even begun to repent." [47]
"Perfection," declares St. Isaac, "is the depth of humility." [48]

In his *Letters to the Ashram,* Gandhi correctly opposes humility
to inertia: "True humility requires . . . the most arduous and constant effort." [49] Humility, for Baudoin the psychologist, has a
biological role and a function of adaptation; it puts us in our
place.[50]

Humility lives "the communion of sinners", this other aspect
that is inseparable from "the communion of saints". While he was
dying, a fool in Christ said: "That all may be saved, that the whole

---

[43] *P.G.,* 88, 816D.
[44] *P.G.,* 94, 976A.
[45] St. Isaac, Wensinck, *op. cit.,* p. 310.
[46] *Lettre,* 185.
[47] *P.G.,* 65, 396.
[48] *Homélie* 78.
[49] *Etudes Carm.* (1947), p. 183.
[50] Quoted by O. Clement, *L'Eglise Orthodoxe* (Paris, 1961), p. 122.

world be saved." Another, at the end of a life of scorn and persecution, affirmed that he had not met a truly bad man.

Today, in countries where life is placed under the sign of the cross and silence, humility becomes the spirituality of martyrs. Its grandeur shines forth in its astonishing hymns of praise. It gives thanks to God even for suffering and persecution, even placing the demons in the hands of God. Having reached the end of what is supportable, man can only say: "Glory be to God," and redouble his prayer for the living and the dead, for the victims and the executioners. It is then that he espouses the heart of God and understands the ineffable.

Christ has come to "awaken the living and change death into a sleep of expectation", into vigils of the spirit. The living are on the other side of death and the dead are the living; such is the joyous revelation of Christian faith, its royal charism.

2. *The Charism of "Joyful Dying"*

If it is true, as Plato says, that "of death there is no knowledge", if it is probable that the future reserves for us both sadness and joy, unforeseen and problematic events, the only absolutely certain thing that awaits us is death; this fact is universal and indisputable.

Heidegger had the courage to put it in the center of his philosophy. It alone radically limits human freedom. Therefore, with this in the background, man must understand himself.

Modern pedagogy, and this is very indicative of its mentality, never speaks of death. It seems to be directed at "immortal" children; it is afraid to touch upon the mystery of death except with decorations, trimmings and lies.

Forgetfulness of death characterizes the world; with great artfulness everything is designed toward this, as if modern man could not bear the idea of it imposed too brutally; as if behind the statement that "all men are mortal", there is hidden an unavowed and senseless thought, an obscure desire that there may be perhaps some exceptions, that this end does not immediately concern me, and in all events, it is never the opportune moment to think of it.

We bury the dead with uneasiness, almost in secret, rapidly, discreetly. The dead are spoilsports; they disturb those who are enjoying life. Certain cemeteries in their almost hideous monotony give the horrible idea of a death that has become industrialized as it were, and of forgetfulness in the anonymity of a common fate. For those who remember, their memories refer to what no longer exists; the poetry of their sadness comes from a dead past. On the contrary, memory itself depends on life, and it keeps the past entirely present. Each one of the dead is a singular and irreplaceable being, living eternally in the memory of God. The Church in her prayers for the dead asks this of God, as she asks also for the grace of the *constant remembrance* of death. St. Benedict's rule prescribes having it before one's eyes every day.

In existentialism, death conditions the famous "transcendence", but the latter is proved to be powerless since it does not transcend death. It is the living being who is transcendent toward death (*Sein zum Tode*). Certainly, such a dialectic vigorously presents the problem, but at the same time it shows its insufficiency. The end and nothingness are granted, but no light is shed here on the meaning of death. A stoppage or lessening of reflection such as this leads one at the most to say: the one who wishes nothingness will have it. Simone de Beauvoir fails when she tries "to conjure death with words".[51] True transcendence ought to affirm the contrary: it is not life that is a phenomenon of death, but it is death that is an episodic and passing phenomenon of life. Only in this perspective does death receive a significance that is luminous in meaning.

The profound pessimism of Freud and Heidegger appears to have been formed naturally, as soon as we reflect on life in relation to its end. To recognize and to accept this end is already a deep and true philosophic attitude, for as Julien Green remarks: "No one speaks so well of life as death does." Indeed an infinite duration in the conditions of this earthly life, time being cut off from its ending, would deprive existence of all meaning. In *Tous les hommes sont mortels* Simone de Beauvoir is in accord with Berdyaev and expresses a just intuition: the indefinite duration of biological ex-

[51] *La Force de l'âge,* p. 617.

istence would culminate in infinite boredom. We can add that the horror of an infernal fate comes exactly from such a boredom being made eternal. For the Fathers of the Church, life without end in earthly conditions could only be a demoniacal nightmare. The love of God for his creatures hinders the eternalization of such a state of life that would be only a suspended death.

The meaning of history, even its possibility, is in direct relation to its end, its balance sheet, its transcendence, more inevitable than death itself toward "the wholly other". "The last enemy to be destroyed will be death," [52] St. Paul energetically declares. The final evil is pregnant with the ultimate solution of the human condition. Death, "the king of terrors", according to Job, causes legitimate anguish, puts a stop to what is habitually profaned by forgetfulness, and in its depth *strikes in all cases* by the greatness of its mystery. At the beginning of his life, St. Augustine wept for the death of a friend, confessing: "Having become an enigma to myself, I questioned my soul." [53]

The value of a human being is measured by his attitude toward death. Plato taught that philosophy was the art of dying well, but philosophy does not know of the victory over death; it can postulate it, but it cannot teach *how* one must die in the resurrection. It only affirms, and in this is its greatness, that time cannot contain eternity, that time without its end would be more absurd than death, and that this world which kills Socrates the Just is not the true world. Even more, its crimes testify to another world where justice reigns, and where Socrates lives forever young and beautiful. For St. Justin, the fate of Socrates prefigured the destiny of Christ who died and rose and in whom Socrates was born again for eternity.

Death is not an instant; it coexists and accompanies man all along the path of his life. It is present in all things as their evident limit. Time and space, instants that vanish and distances that separate, are so many breaks or partial deaths. Every goodbye, change, forgetfulness, the fact that nothing can ever be reproduced exactly—all bring the breath of death even to the heart of life and rock us in anguish. Every departure of a loved one, the end of

[52] 1 Cor. 15, 26.
[53] *Conf.,* 4, 4.

every passion, the traces of time on a human face, the last look at a city or a landscape that we shall never see again, or simply a faded flower—all arouse a profound melancholy, an immediate experience of our anticipated death.

Nature does not know any personal immortality; it knows only the survival of the species. Atheists can dream only of survival in their works or in the memory of the generations to come; it is a dreary dictionary-immortality at best.

The virulence of death can be neutralized only by its own negation. That is why the cross is raised in the center of the world, and life freely accepts passing through death in order to shatter it and bring it to nothingness. "By death, you have conquered death," sings the Church on the Vigil of Easter. Origen reports a tradition according to which the body of Adam was buried where Christ was crucified.[54] Another tradition has it that the wood of the cross had its origin in a tree in Eden. The Bible knows nothing of natural immortality and reveals the resurrection as coming from beyond— from the death and resurrection of the God-Man. Thus Christianity *alone* accepts the tragedy of death, and looks at it face to face, for God has passed along that road and all follow him.

If philosophy brings knowledge of death, Christian ascesis offers the art of going beyond it and thus anticipating the resurrection. Indeed, death is entirely in time. For those around a dying person, his death is dated, but for the one who has just died, it has no date, for he already finds himself in another dimension. Just as the end of the world will have no earthly tomorrow, death is not a day on the calendar for anyone; this is why the death of each one, like the end of the world, is *for today*. Likewise it is not tomorrow but the very day of the eucharistic repast when one enters into the kingdom.

For a man whose spirit has been rendered immortal, the non-existence of death is evident, because it is on this side, while he is on the other. As an element of time, death is behind us; before us is found what has already been experienced in baptism: the "little

[54] *P.G.*, 13, 1777. The icon of the crucifixion shows Adam's skull at the foot of the cross. The chapel of Adam in the Church of the Holy Sepulcher in Jerusalem bears the inscription: "The place of the skull has become paradise."

resurrection", and in the eucharist: life eternal. The one who follows Christ "does not come to judgment, but has passed from death to life". "The one who eats my flesh and drinks my blood has eternal life." The final reality of ourselves lives on the threshold of this paschal passage; the act of faith discovers it and sees things "that are not seen", according to St. Paul.

"If anyone comes to me and does not hate . . . even his own life, he cannot be my disciple." [55] Thus, to hate means to oppose an obstacle, an excessive attachment to life here below or a fear of death —all of which makes the spirit captive. To a thoughtful man, death deprived of anguish manifests his own grandeur and nobility. It purifies and despoils the dead of what is merely accessory, inclines us to keep "a good memory" of them, to appreciate them in a disinterested way, to rectify the scale of values beyond time and in the face of eternity. The face of a dead person has for some moments a peaceful and majestic spiritual beauty: "that impenetrable smile of the dead which is in such harmony with their marvelous silence." [56] The presence of death has something august about it; it ennobles our feelings, and during a brief instant makes each one truer and greater. The death of another is a trial, and the one who experiences this receives the dignity of surviving and of preparing himself for the mystery of his own accounting.

Normally death is the time of harvest for a life "laden with days", and ripe for eternity. According to the beautiful words of ancient martyrologies, it is the *die natalis,* the birthday, and only God knows this day and the hour. The words of Pascal, "One dies alone," [57] and those of Kierkegaard, "That I die is not a generality for me," [58] mean that each one of us totally assumes his death. Man is the priest of his death; he is what he makes of his death. The last anointing admirably introduces us into this priesthood, offering "an oil of gladness" and an exaltation of heart above the agony of the body.

Diadochus [59] remarks that grave illnesses take the place of

[55] Luke 14, 26.
[56] Bernanos, *Journal d'un curé de campagne* (Ed. Pléiade), p. 1167.
[57] British Edition, p. 211.
[58] *Post-Scriptum,* II, p. 110.
[59] Chap. 94.

martyrdom. Even more, to *each one* is given the grace, the charism of martyrdom, when, in the face of death that replaces the executioner, man can still call it "our Sister Death", and confess the *Credo*, evidence that he has already passed from death to life (cf. Col. 2, 12; John 5, 24). Great spiritual men have often lain in their own coffins, as if they were in a nuptial bed, manifesting a brotherly familiarity, an intimacy with death, that is only a passage and a definitive point of departure. Erasmus observed this intimacy in the saints and thought it constituted a second nature that had dislodged the first.

St. Seraphin of Sarov used to teach "joyful dying". "For us, to die will be a joy," he was accustomed to say to his disciples. That is why he addressed each person he met with the paschal salutation: "My joy, Christ is risen"; death is non-existent and life reigns.

In his letter to the Corinthians, St. Paul presents an astounding vision: "All things are yours . . . life or death . . . all are yours," [60] both with the same claim.

3. *Prayer*

    The State of Prayer

    "Pray without ceasing," [61] insists St. Paul, for prayer is at the same time the source and the most intimate form of our life. "When thou prayest, go into thy room, and closing the door, pray to thy Father in secret." [62] This means to enter into yourself and make a sanctuary there; the secret place is the human heart. The life of prayer, its intensity, its depth, its rhythm are a measure of our spiritual health and reveal ourselves to ourselves.

    "Rising up long before daybreak, he went out and departed into a desert place, and there he prayed." [63] With the ascetics, "the desert" is interiorized and signifies the concentration of a recollected and silent spirit. At this level, where man knows how to be silent, true prayer is found; here he is mysteriously visited. Paul

---

[60] 1 Cor. 3, 21-22.
[61] 1 Thess, 5, 17.
[62] Matt. 6, 6.
[63] Mark 1, 35.

Claudel notes that the Word is the adopted son of silence, for St. Joseph passes through the pages of the Gospel without uttering a single word. To hear the voice of the Word, we must know how to listen to his silence, and above all, to learn it ourselves. Speaking from experience, the spiritual masters are categorical: if one does not know how to give a place in his life to recollection and silence, it is impossible for him to arrive at a higher degree and to be able to pray in public places. This degree makes us aware that one part of us, being immersed in what is immediate, is always worried and distracted, and that the other part observes this with astonishment and compassion. A man too busy with many things would make the angels laugh, if they could do so, Shakespeare remarks.[64]

The water that quenches thirst is distilled in the silence that offers us the indispensable withdrawal to view ourselves in the right perspective.

Recollection opens our soul to heaven, but also to other men. St. Seraphin states admirably: the contemplative life *or* the active life—this problem is somewhat artificial; this is not the problem; the real problem is that of the heart's dimension. Is the vast jewel case, of which Origen speaks, capable of containing God and all men? If so, St. Seraphin says: "Acquire interior peace, and a multitude of men will find their salvation near you." [65]

There are evident realities in the world, the kingdom, for example, and there are symbols also. "The kingdom of heaven is like . . .", and then comes the idea, the theory, which is a certain impoverishment. That is why poetry, and even more, prayer, is nearer truth than is prose. Lao-tse used to say that if he had absolute power, he would before all else reestablish the initial poetic meaning of words. In this present time of verbal inflation that only aggravates loneliness, only the man of prayerful peace can still speak to others, and show them the word become a face and a look become a presence. His silence will speak where no preaching can reach; his mystery will make others attentive to a revelation that has now become close and accessible to them. Even when he who knows silence speaks, he easily finds the unsullied freshness of every

[64] *Measure for Measure*, Act. II, scene 2.
[65] *Révélations de saint Séraphin*.

word. His answer to questions of life and death comes as the *amen* to his perpetual prayer.

St. Teresa used to say: "To pray means to treat God like a friend." The "friend of the bridegroom . . . stands and hears him".[66] The essence of the state of prayer is to hear the voice of another, that of Christ, but likewise that of the person I meet, in whom Christ addresses me. His voice comes to me in every human voice; his face is multiple: it is that of the wayfarer to Emmaus of Mary Magdalen's gardener, of my next-door neighbor. God became incarnate so that man may contemplate his face through every face. Perfect prayer seeks the presence of Christ and recognizes it in every human being. The unique image of Christ is the icon, but they are innumerable, and this means that every human face is also the icon of Christ. A prayerful attitude discovers it.

The Degrees of Prayer

In the beginning, prayer is agitated and silence is inwardly talkative. In the words of Péguy, we should not pray like geese waiting for their mash! Being emotional, man pours out all the contents of his mind; before he feels weariness from this monologue, the spiritual writers advise occupying his time in reciting the psalms and in reading. St. John Climacus condemns prolixity: "No affectation in the words of your prayer. How many times the simple and monotonous stammerings of his children move a father. Do not throw yourself into long speeches so as not to dissipate your mind in a search for words. A single word of the publican touched the mercy of God; a single word, full of faith, saved the good thief. Long-windedness and talkativeness in prayer fill the mind with images and distract it, while often a single word has the effect of recollecting it." [67] "It is not necessary to use many words; it is sufficient to keep one's hands elevated," says St. Macarius.[68] In Chapter XX of his *Rule*, St. Benedict declares: "It is not in the abundance of words that we shall be heard, but by the compunction of our tears."

[66] John 3, 29.
[67] *The Heavenly Ladder,* degree 28.
[68] *P.G.,* 34, 249.

The Lord's Prayer is very brief. A hermit on Mount Athos used to begin this prayer at sunset and end it saying *Amen* to the rays of the rising sun. Talking is not the question; it is a question of fully living the entire worlds created by each word of our prayer. Great spiritual men are satisfied with pronouncing the name of Jesus, but in this name they contemplate the kingdom.

If a man understands this lesson, he rectifies his attitude, making it agree with the liturgical aspiration: "Make of my prayer a sacrament of your presence." Man should lend an ear to the voice of God. St. Seraphin counsels: "We ought to pray until the Holy Spirit descends upon us . . . When he has come to visit us, we cease praying."

With modern man the difficulty comes from the separation of the intellect from the heart, of knowledge from value judgments. Ancient tradition suggests: "In the morning place your intellect in your heart and remain all day in the company of God." In other words, render the divided elements of your being coherent and thus regain integrity of spirit. An ancient prayer asks: "By your love, bind my soul," that from the aggregate of my states of soul, a single soul may spring forth.

A serious deformation makes prayer the mechanical repetition of formulas and of texts that have been learned. True prayer changes into a constant attitude, into a state of mind that structures and molds our whole being liturgically. Here is seen the great truth that to *have* is still a symbol, the reality is to *be*. According to spiritual writers, it is not enough to *have* prayers, rules, habits; one must *be* prayer incarnate.[69] It is in his very structure that man sees himself as a liturgical being, as the man of the *Sanctus,* the one who by his whole life and his whole being prostrates and adores, one who can say: "I sing praise to my God while I live." [70] To make of one's life a liturgy, a prayer, a doxology, is to make of it a sacrament of perpetual communion. "God descends to the soul in prayer and the spirit rises to God."[71]

[69] Origen, *P.G.,* 11, 452C-D; St. Basil, *P.G.,* 31, 244A.
[70] Ps. 104, 33.
[71] St. John Damascene, *P.G.,* 94, 1089.

The elevation of man corresponds to the abasement of God. Léon Bloy tells of an old man who constantly walked bareheaded, for he always felt himself in the presence of God. A very expressive image of a prayerful attitude has become one's very life. St. Paul relates it to the act of faith. "Put your own selves to the test, whether you are in the faith; prove yourselves. Do you not know yourselves that Christ Jesus is in you." [72]

Though it is an act, faith rejects all formalism which soon creeps into exterior prayers, into routine duties absent of thought, likewise into all tacit complacency in mystic experiences where man is too much present. "Prayer is not perfect if man is conscious of himself and perceives that he is praying." [73]

Faith invites us to follow Christ naked even in his sacerdotal prayer which is the liturgy of universal intercession.

The Forms of Prayer

The Lord taught authentic prayer in the Sermon on the Mount. The disciples asked him: "Teach us to pray," and Christ gave the gift of the *Our Father*.

All prayer comes from three forms—request, offering, praise. We find all three in the Lord's Prayer: "Give us this day our daily bread", "forgive us our trespasses", "deliver us from evil"; then, "thy will be done on earth as it is in heaven", "thy kingdom come", which means "Accept the offering of our lives for this end; accept our pardon of others and make us thy servants and thy witnesses." Finally, "Hallowed be thy name"; "for thine is the kingdom, the power and the glory."

St. Basil in his *Monastic Constitutions* advises: "Begin to say humbly: 'I am a sinner; I give you thanks, Lord, for having patiently borne with me . . .' Then ask for the reign of God and then for respectable things, and do not cease until you have obtained them."

We can recognize these three forms in the responses to liturgical litanies. In the story of a tanner who learned humility from St.

---

[72] 2 Cor. 13, 5.
[73] Cassian, *Confer.*, IX, 31.

Anthony, in the description of his prayer, we see he followed them exactly and thus showed how these forms become a state of prayer sanctifying all moments, even for those who do not have any particular time for prayer at their disposal. In the morning this workman presented all the inhabitants of Alexandria to God, saying "Have pity on us sinners." During the day, his soul did not cease to think of his work as an offering: "For thee, Lord." In the evening, being very happy that he had been kept in life, he could say only: "Glory to thee."

Among the faithful Jews, the law was graven on their hearts, always present before their eyes, written on their hands. Their entire being was thus structured by the law; their gaze recognized the law in the life of the world, the creation of divine wisdom; and finally the law was accomplished by their hands, by their everyday acts.

Prayer follows the same universalism; everything is sanctified and blessed by it; everything becomes one of its forms. This is the prayerful conception of life where the most humble labor of a workman and the creation of a genius are equally entitled to be an offering before the face of God, and are received as a task given by the Father.

For the spiritual life it is also a decisive passage from "Jesus before the eyes" to "Jesus in the heart" according to the hesychastic tradition of Jesus' prayer.

The Prayer of Jesus [74]

The prayer called the prayer of Jesus or that of the heart was developed on Mount Athos. Associated with the names of St. Macarius, Diadochus of Photike, St. John Climacus, St. Symeon and all the great spiritual leaders, it originated in the biblical conception of the name.

According to the Bible, the name of God is one of his attributes where he is present and where he shows himself. In a special manner, the invocation of the name of Jesus makes the grace of his

[74] See *La prière de Jésus,* by a monk of the Eastern Church (Chevetogne, 1951). Also *Récit d'un pélerin russe* (Neuchâtel, 1948).

incarnation universal, allowing each man his personal share and
disposing his heart to receive the Lord. The strength of the divine
presence in his name proves its greatness. "See, I am sending an
angel before you, to guard you on the way . . . be attentive to
him . . . for my name is in him." [75]

"My name is in him" and consequently the angel is the bearer
of his formidable presence. When the divine name is pronounced
over a country or a person, these enter into an intimate relationship
with God. The invocation of the name of God is accompanied by
its immediate manifestation, for the name is a form of his presence.
This is why his name could only be pronounced by the great
sacrificer on the day of Yom-Kippur, in "the holy of holies" of the
temple in Jerusalem. The incarnation makes each man a similar
sacrificer, but it is at every moment that he benefits from the name.
The name of Jesus—*Jeshua*—means Savior. *Nomen est Omen;* it
contains in cipher the power of salvation. "The name of the Son
of God sustains the entire world," says Hermas,[76] for he is present
there and we adore him in his name.

The "prayer of the heart" frees and enlarges it, and attracts
Jesus to it by the incessant invocation: "Lord Jesus Christ, Son of
God, have pity on me, a sinner!"

In this prayer, which is that of the publican in the Gospel, the
whole Bible with its entire message is reduced to its essential
simplicity: confession of the Lordship of Jesus, of his divine filia-
tion, therefore, of the trinity; then the fall that called for the abyss
of divine mercy. The beginning and the end are gathered here in a
single word charged with the sacramental presence of Christ in his
name. This prayer ceaselessly resounds in the depths of a man's
soul, even outside his will and consciousness. Finally, the name of
Jesus resounds of itself, taking on the rhythm of the man's respiration, in some way "attached" to his breath; even during sleep:
"I was sleeping, but my heart kept vigil." [77]

When Jesus is drawn into the heart, the liturgy becomes interior
and the kingdom is in the peaceful soul. The name dwells in man
as in its temple, and there the divine presence transmutes and

[75] Ex. 23, 20.
[76] *Pastor,* III, 14.
[77] Cant. 5, 2.

Christifies him. This was the experience of St. Paul, whom we can better understand in the light of this prayer: "It is no longer I that live, but Christ lives in me."

At the present time, a great number of believers of all confessions find an efficacious help in this essentially biblical practice that proves to be a privileged ecumenical means of unity and of encountering the name of Jesus.

"There are powerful beings like St. Michael, but for us, the weak, there remains nothing but to take refuge in the name of Jesus," confesses St. Barsanuphius.[78] St. John Climacus adds: "Strike your adversary with the name of Jesus; there is no more powerful weapon on the earth or in the skies." [79]

The invocation of the name of Jesus is within the reach of every man in all the circumstances of his life. It places the name as a divine seal on everything, and makes the world its dwelling place. By this prayer, the most precious tradition of hesychasm adapts to man, causes to live within him the thousand-year experience of the greatest masters and makes of him a vigilant witness united to all men, giving them comfort and refreshment like a tree or a spring of water.

"Pray for those who do not know how to pray, who do not wish to do so, and especially for those who have never prayed," said the Patriarch Justinian in Rumania in 1953. His exhortation is on the level of the prayer of Jesus.

Liturgical Prayer

The distinction between mental and vocal prayer is very theoretical. For the ancients, psalmody was the natural expression of interior prayer, "the psalmody of the soul".

The prayer of the Church was formed in convents. It provided an admirable rhythm for the day and night of a monastic community. The people did not participate in it except on Sundays and feast days; this imposed on the laity an effort to interiorize it in

[78] Correspondence of Barsanuphius and John. See *La prière de Jésus*, p. 26-27.
[79] *The Heavenly Ladder*, degree 27.

order that they might find themselves in the same prayerful rhythm through their hours of work and toil in the world.

In the beginning, the eucharist was celebrated only on Sunday, the day of the Lord. The weekdays brought matins, vespers and the other hours, following the prayer of the synagogue. It was a prayer of praise extended throughout the week, and a thanksgiving inspired by the *mirabilia Dei*.

The blessing on the day means that each day man restores to all things their biblical meaning: to be creatures of God, destined to praise him. "Not rendering evil . . . but contrariwise blessing, for unto this were you called." [80]

In the evening, the blessing on the night expresses the astonishment of man that, in spite of his failures, he is still living and can thank God for having helped him. The day just spent is thus presented as a particle of sacred history, of the divine economy of salvation in which man has accomplished the task entrusted to him by God. It receives an accent of eternity, and as the ear of wheat, it carries the sun in each of its grains and bends under the weight of its own fullness.

Terce, Sext, None, marking the ninth, twelfth and fifteenth hours of the day, effect a triple return to God in the midst of human occupations, a pause that opens time upon its liturgical and heavenly dimension. The offices of *Prime* and *Compline,* which begin and end the day, have their last chord in the middle of the night with the *Nocturns,* which are the vigils of the spirit, the watchful waiting of the wise virgins in order not to forget themselves and not to forget the bridegroom who is already coming and is now at the door.

St. John Chrysostom speaks profoundly of the Christian house as a place of prayer that makes it an *ecclesia domestica.* "Let your house be a church; rise in the middle of the night. During the night, the soul is purer and less heavy. Adore your master. If you have children, wake them and let them unite with you in a common prayer." [81] Even those who waste time or kill it are included in the vigils of those who pray in this way. They present to God men's cares and their thoughtlessness, their suffering, their sorrows and

[80] 1 Peter 3, 9.
[81] *Hom. sur les Actes,* 26, 3-4.

their joys. Every instant of our time is rejuvenated and refreshed by this contact with the ardor of those praying. The wild movements of the hands of the clock stop at the immovable noon of love, and on the dial of the liturgical mysteries time is reordered and redeemed. Time is directed toward its own end. Each of its rhythmic moments appears full of meaning and creativity; it preaches and sings of the kingdom.

Liturgical Prayer, the Rule of All Prayer

The prayer of the Church bears the vibrations of biblical revelation; it comes from the totality of truth and has its culmination there. That is why every rule of prayer begins with an invocation of the Trinity and includes the confession of the *Credo*.

If the needs of the time naturally inspire individual prayer, on the other hand, liturgical prayer loses this note of the particular and introduces us at once into a colloquial consciousness—according to the word, *liturgy,* which means work in common. It teaches the true relationship between myself and others, and makes us understand the words: "Love thy neighbor as thyself." It helps us to be detached from ourselves and to make ours the prayer of humanity.

The litanies lead the individual beyond himself, toward the assembly, toward those who are absent, those who suffer, and finally those who are in their agony. Prayer embraces the city, nations, humanity, and asks for peace and union for all. All isolation, all individualistic separation, sounds a false note in this perfect harmony. Formed liturgically, every soul knows by experience that he cannot stand alone before God and that, liturgically, he saves himself with others. The pronoun in the liturgy is never in the singular.

The liturgy filters out every subjective, emotional and fleeting tendency. Full of a healthy and powerful affective life, it offers us its finished form, made perfect by long centuries and by all the generations that have prayed in the same way. As the walls of the church bear the imprint of all the prayers, offerings and intercessions, the liturgical prayers across hundreds of years are the breath of innumerable human lives. I hear the voice of St. John Chrysostom, St. Basil, St. Simeon, and so many others who have prayed the same prayers and have left in them their adoring spirit; they help me to find their ardor and to associate myself with their prayers.

However, if the liturgy gives the measure and the rule of all prayer, it also calls for spontaneous and personal prayer in which the soul sings and speaks freely to the Lord. The liturgy teaches it, in calling each one by name as if he were the only one, and each one is called upon to profess the *Credo,* I believe. Even in the framework of the liturgy, this profession puts stress on the most personal act possible; no one can do it in my place. The liturgical texts are attuned to the soul and impel it to a direct and intimate conversation that keeps all its own value.

Difficulties and Obstacles

The most frequent difficulty, one that everybody knows, is to harmonize our psychic world—its changing content, agitated and burdened with the cares of the present—with the content of liturgical prayer or with our personal obligation. Behind the very real tension of seeking harmony, there is often hidden a secret resistance, a very refined form of temptation. It generally advances the argument of sincerity: We do not find ourselves just now in the state of prayer; in forcing ourselves we risk profaning what is sacred, for in every way we would remain distracted, exterior, and in the end, boredom, and lassitude would triumph. Should we really in this case wait for the moment of inspiration, with the risk that we shall never find it?

To suppress this form of temptation at the very outset, and to avoid all misunderstanding, it is important to grasp the fact that prayer requires a preliminary state, an ascetic *effort.*

Here is the experience of a hermit: "I believe there is nothing so painful as prayer. When a man begins to pray, then his enemies, the demons, try to hinder him from it . . . Prayer requires that we fight to the last sigh." [82]

There is also the natural resistance that comes from laziness and

---

[82] *Apophtegmata.* See Stolz, *L'Ascèse chrétienne,* p. 159.

heaviness of soul. This darkened side of human nature makes us understand the words of Origen: "A single saint by his prayer is stronger in his struggle than a crowd of sinners." [83] Elsewhere this author notes the fact that climbing up a high mountain is fatiguing.[84]

Prayer thus possesses its own struggle. It is no stranger to that "violence" that bears away the kingdom, violence to man whom it casts to the ground in adoration, violence to God in making him incline toward earth and the man in prayer.[85]

"By his death, he has conquered death." Likewise every prayer entails its own cross, and by its effort it conquers effort so that finally it springs forth freely and joyfully. The body conditions the effort; fasting, genuflections, prostrations help the spirit to concentrate, attuning it as a musical instrument.

The masters tell us that we must go beyond the first difficult moment by attentively reading the psalms; to act "as if" inspiration were not lacking, and then the miracle of grace will operate. Ambrose of Optino, a staret, has said: "Read a chapter of the Gospel every day; and when anxiety seizes you, read again until it passes away; if it returns, read the Gospel once more." [86]

The Fathers teach that the Holy Spirit is the only *gift* which, once requested, never remains without an immediate answer. It is the *epiklesis* of prayer, the invocation that reaches the very nature of the one who is giving himself and impels him to manifest himself.

Why pray? Does not God know what we need? This objection is aimed at the prayer of request and intercession. The Gospel makes no distinction between the forms of prayer and states clearly: "If two of you shall agree on earth about anything at all for which they ask, it shall be done for them by my Father." [87]

One cannot unite except in a third, in the will of God who desires unity, and then, according to the Gospel, such unity moves

---

[83] *Hom. in Num.*, 25, 2.

[84] *P.G.*, 12, 743B.

[85] "The Master inclined toward earth and found his image" (N. Cabasilas, *La Vie en Jésus-Christ*, p. 28).

[86] P. Tchetverikov, *Optino* (Paris, 1926), in Russian.

[87] John 15, 16; Matt. 18, 19.

the will of the Father. God listens to our prayer, he rectifies it and makes it an element added to his decision. The violent insistence of the widow of the Gospel wrung a response that makes the power of prayer stand out clearly. St. Paul begged the Lord three times to remove the sting from his flesh. The life of St. Seraphin gives an account of the prayer of a saint for the soul of a condemned sinner. Day and night the saint was in prayer; he struggled with divine justice, and though struck by lightning, his ardent prayer in its very boldness caused the mercy of God to triumph, and the sinner was pardoned. Perhaps hell depends also on the violence of the charity of saints, and God may expect that our prayers may bring about the *apocatastasis* (final blessedness).

Have we enough time to pray? Certainly, and much more than we think. "How many moments of torpor, of inattention, could become instants of prayer, so that we might become vigilant, attentive to persons and things—even worry, if it is expressed in dialogue with God, in contestation, in abandonment. We can even offer the exhaustion that hinders prayer and even our powerlessness to pray." [88]

In these frequent states of loneliness and weariness, the name of Jesus can become an interior appeal during a conversation, a light that illumines a monotonous work, a sound of reality that dispels reverie, in short, a simple blessing on persons and things.[89] "The remembrance of God, without formulating a single word, is already a prayer and a help," [90] says St. Barsanuphius.

However, "in the hours when the mind wanders, it is better to attach oneself by preference to reading rather than to prayer", until the moment when "the Spirit himself will teach the heart".[91] That is why, St. Isaac explains: "Prayer is the key that opens the understanding to the Scriptures." [92]

[88] O. Clément, "Témoignage de la foi," in *Contacts* (1961), nos. 35-36, p. 246.
[89] *Ibid.*
[90] *Philocalie* (in Russian), vol. II, 584.
[91] St. Isaac, Wensinck, *op. cit.*, p. 299, 62.
[92] *Ibid.*, p. 220.

4
Lectio Divina:
Reading the Bible

"May the sun on rising find you with a Bible in your hand." [93] This exclamation of Evagrius well expresses the patristic tradition. Canon 19 of the Council of Trullo enjoined priests to initiate the faithful into the greatest intimacy with the Bible. St. John Chrysostom vigorously insists: "I am not a monk, some of you say . . . But your mistake is in believing that the reading of the Scriptures concerns only monks, because *for you it is still more necessary* since you are in the midst of the world. There is something worse than not reading the Scriptures, and that is to believe that this reading is useless . . . a satanic practice." [94]

"Having returned from church, the husband should repeat what has been read; one will thus prepare a spiritual repast, as well as a material one." [95] The saint counsels studying at home the passage that is to be read in church so that the children will be accustomed to a daily and attentive reading of Holy Scripture.[96]

For Origen,[97] such reading is not simply an exercise added to one's daily life, it is an organic part of one's spiritual life, transforming the day into a living reading of the Word, where the Word himself speaks unceasingly. It directs the struggle and the progress of the soul; by this reading the soul becomes an *anima ecclesiastica,* and man, according to Clement of Alexandria,[98] becomes a "theodidact" (taught by God).

[93] *P.G.,* 40, 1283A.
[94] *Hom. in Matth.,* 2, 5.
[95] *In Gen. Serm.,* 6, 2.
[96] *In Ephes.,* 21, 2-3.
[97] *P.G.,* 13, 166.
[98] *Strom.,* 1, 20.

In the Rule of St. Pachomius, Scripture is to nourish the mind of the monks all day long. During the hours of work, they sing and recite the sacred writings; in the evening, all are together in order to listen to the commentaries. The recitation of the Scriptures by heart was a common practice. For St. Nil, hunger for the Scriptures was the measure of our spiritual being.[99] For St. Isaac: "The constant meditation on the Word is the light of the soul." [100]

All spiritual writers sound a warning—never profane the Word by making it an object of speculation or of knowledge for the sake of knowledge, for "to understand what we read is a grace from God".[101] Hermas teaches that ascesis and prayer are like a question to which the Lord answers by a revelation of the meaning of the Scriptures.[102] Likewise a troparion (hymn) of *None* says: "Between the two thieves, thy cross appeared as a balance of justice, one of the scales sinking toward hell with the weight of blasphemy, the other becoming lighter with the loss of sins through knowing the divine Word."

Reading presupposes then "the state of prayer" that brings words to maturity. "Prayer causes God to illumine man's mind in order that it can grasp what he reads." God became man "in order to be closer to us than our own soul", and to give us "the same mind which was in Christ Jesus".[103] That is why for Nicolas Cabasilas, "the Gospel *figures* Christ",[104] which means that it lets Christ speak by himself, inviting us to fill our eyes and hearts with "the one who attracts to himself alone and unites to himself alone".[105] For St. Justin, the Scriptures effect a decisive encounter,[106] and every martyr by his death testifies that he has read them correctly.

The essential method of reading the Scriptures, according to Nicodemus the Hagiorite, is to go "from the written word to the

[99] *P.G.,* 79, 213C.
[100] Wensinck, *op. cit.,* p. 61.
[101] St. Symeon, *Discourse on the Scriptures, P.G.,* 120, 385.
[102] *Vision* II, 1-4.
[103] Phil. 2, 5.
[104] *Expl. de la div. liturgie,* 412C; 416B.
[105] *Ibid.,* 501A.
[106] *Dialogue,* 91, 94.

substantial Word", and it is in this passage, decisive for the spiritual life, that the patristic commentaries appear to be sure guides.

The Fathers of the Church lived the Bible; they thought and spoke by the Bible, with that admirable penetration which went even to the identification of their being with the biblical substance itself. If one tries to learn from them, one understands that the word read and heard leads always to the living person of the Word. St. John Chrysostom prayed before the Holy Book: "Lord Jesus Christ, open the eyes of my heart so that I may understand and fulfill thy will . . . illumine my eyes by thy light." Likewise St. Ephrem advised: "Before every reading, pray and supplicate God that *he may reveal himself to you.*" St. Athanasius declared: "In the words of Scripture the Lord is found, whose presence the demons cannot stand." [107]

We can say that for the Fathers, the Bible *is* Christ, for each of its words puts us in his presence: "Him whom I seek in books," confessed St. Augustine.[108]

Clement of Alexandria shows that we must nourish ourselves on the seeds of life contained in the Bible as we do in the eucharist.[109] It is Origen who fixed the meaning of the "eating" of the Scriptures,[110] and tradition has followed him. We consume "eucharistically" the "Word mysteriously broken".[111] St. Jerome says: "We eat his flesh and drink his blood in the divine eucharist, but also in the reading of Scripture." [112] St. Gregory of Nazianzen compares the reading of the Bible to the consummation of the paschal lamb.

This eucharistic manner of consuming the Word presupposes the *epiklesis* of every reading. The Word is living by the Spirit that rests in it, as he placed himself over the Son in his epiphany. We must read it then in the dimension of the Paraclete, which is that of the body of Christ, of the Church and of tradition in which the

[107] *P.G.,* 27, 45.
[108] *Confes.* II, 2.
[109] *Strom.,* 1, 1.
[110] *P.G.,* 13, 130-134.
[111] Origen, *P.G.,* 13, 1734; see also St. John Chrysostom, *In Gen. Serm.,* 6, 2; St. Gregory Nazianzen, *Oratio,* 45, 16.
[112] *In Eccles.,* 3, 13.

Word speaks. God willed that Christ form the body where his words resound as words of life; it is then in Christ, within him, in the Church that we must read and listen. The Church alone keeps the Word, for as Origen teaches,[113] she possesses the Spirit that has dictated it.

At the time of the liturgy, the people are convoked first to hear and then to consume the Word. This hearing builds up the People of God, forms the eucharistic preparation for consuming the Word incarnate, and for entering into substantial communion with the Word.

St. Luke's Gospel tells us [114] that Christ opened the minds of his disciples, in showing them how one must read the Bible in order to discover there all that was written concerning him, and how, beginning with Moses and all the prophets, he explained to them what was written of him in all the Scriptures. It was thus that the Lord opened the meaning of the Scriptures and revealed that the entire Bible is *the verbal icon of Christ*.

In reading the Scriptures we can discern the prefigurative and the typological meaning, and the accomplishment of the prophecies in the messianic period of the coming of Christ. We can grasp also the historic and eschatological meaning and the accomplishment of history in leading to the kingdom. However, it is the liturgy that offers the method of ecclesial meditation in which the Word is proclaimed, sung, prayed and experienced. The liturgy is prolonged in the life of the faithful and is found again in the daily *lectio divina,* which continues to be a form of prayer and of communion. Here God speaks, intervenes in the life of every man, and invites him to take to the road in company with the angels and saints. Such reading is at the source of its being and is its end. According to St. John Chrysostom, the reading of Scripture is the priesthood of the laity that leads them to sanctity.

That is why in every reading and meditation we must avoid the fearful dryness of reasoning and suppress also emotional dreaming. We can easily make a cadaver out of a text; we cannot give it life, for this comes from the presence of God.

[113] *In Matt.,* 14.
[114] Luke 24, 45.

We can read the Bible in a continuous manner, extended over a year; we can choose one book or follow a theme through all the books; we can meditate on a verse or a single word. Each method is good, if it nourishes our spiritual life. Contemplation is added to the understanding. A description evokes historical realities, contemplation grasps their silent depths. Starting from history, every true reading contemplates the icon of the kingdom.

Thus, reading opens the way to God,[115] but it imposes also the duty of communicating to others the revealed message.[116] The *lectio divina* leads to the apostolate, for "the Word", according to St. Paul, consists "in the demonstration of the Spirit and of power".[117]

[115] Hermas, *Simil.* VIII, 6, 7.
[116] *Ibid.*, X, 4.
[117] 1 Cor. 2, 4.

5
Universal Priesthood of the Laity in the Eastern Tradition

The Greek translation of the Hebrew texts of the Old Testament (such as the Aquila version) applies the word *laikos*—profane or lay—not to men but to things, for example, a "profane land", a "profane journey". "The profane" or "common bread" [118] (*bebēlos* in the Septuagint, *laices panes* in the Vulgate) are "profane things" that are not destined for the service of the temple.[119]

The first Christian document that mentions the word "lay" is the letter to the Corinthians, said to be by St. Clement of Rome (ca. 95 A.D.). It speaks of the conduct of men of the people according to "lay rules". From the 3rd century, with Tertullian and St. Cyprian in North Africa, the term "lay" takes its place beside that of "cleric". Here there is already a juridical interpretation that opposes "lay" to "cleric". Finally we find with St. Jerome (the beginning of the 5th century) not a definition but a clearly pejorative statement: opposite the clergy, those set aside for the things of God, are the lay people, those who look after the things of this world, who marry, carry on business, cultivate the land, testify in court.

If in the Bible the word "lay" is rare and somewhat vague, it contains, however, a very rich and clear notion of the *laos,* the People of God. At the side of a functional priesthood (the levitical, priestly caste), Scripture speaks of the universal priesthood of the People of God in its totality. Since the giving of the Torah to Moses, the Lord declares: "You shall be a kingdom of priests (*mamleket kohanim*), a holy nation." [120] The Greek text translates it as *basileion hierateuma,* a royal priesthood, a "people of priests" in

---

[118] 1 Sam. 21, 4 (1 Kings 21, 4)
[119] 1 Sam 21, 5-6 (1 Kings 21, 5-6); Ezek. 48, 15.
[120] Ex. 19, 6.

195

the service of the heavenly king. In the New Testament, St. Peter takes up the expression, "You are a chosen race, a royal priesthood." [121] The People of God, set apart and formerly united to the temple of Jerusalem, is now associated with the *acta et passa Christi in carne*. From the prophetic regime, the people now constituted as the Church pass to the revealed reality. Henceforth they are united in Christ and share in the unique priesthood and royalty of Jesus. Christ has made of all Christians "a kingdom and priests, and they shall reign over the earth".[122]

The idea of a profane or lay people has no place in the Bible; it would be absolutely unimaginable. The Scriptures teach in a most firm and constant manner the sacred and priestly character of each member of the people.

The first disquieting signs appeared as early as the end of the 4th century—premature fruit of the age of Constantine. It was the lay people themselves who relinquished their dignity as a universal priesthood, and then inevitably the bishops became more and more the point of concentration of the sacred, the priestly, "the consecrated". A distance was formed by the indigence, the progressive impoverishment of the laity, by its terrible refusal of the gifts of the Holy Spirit. This was the great "treason of the laity", a betrayal of their priestly character. Of the two poles of the *laos,* the People of God, one was that of the Christian king who protected the Church and was called "the exterior bishop" and "ecumenical deacon" (title of the Byzantine emperors), and the other was that of the monk, who lived in the things of God. These two poles safeguarded the charismatic dignity of the laity; but the rest, what was between these two poles, fell into a vacuum, now really *profane*. The mass of people, though baptized, was identified with the things of this world, and expressed the Old Testament meaning of the word "lay" that had been applied to things, and became themselves one of the profane things of this world. It is in this state of rapid decadence that the pejorative terms of *biōtikoi* and of *anieroi* are applicable—those who live in the world and are strangers to sacred and holy things. Since then, the definition of the laity is negative.

[121] 1 Peter 2, 9.
[122] Apoc. 5, 10.

A lay person is a passive element of pure receptivity; he has nothing to do *in* the Church (except contribute financially), for he has no ecclesiastical function; he has no ministry or charism.

Now the *Epistle to Diogenetes* (beginning of the 3rd century) affirms: "Each one dwells in his country as a resident foreigner. Every foreign land is to him a fatherland, and every fatherland, a foreign country. He passes his life on earth, but he is a citizen of heaven." This text only accentuates the teaching of St. Paul: the faithful, the laity, are the chosen of God and fellow citizens of the saints; they have here below no lasting city. We can note a dizzy descent from the dignity of "saints" (those called to holiness) to the profane state of those occupied solely with the things of this world. This is an extreme profanation of the sacred.

In the face of this decadence, the true tradition has nevertheless remained unchanging. We find it in the dogmas, in the sacramental and liturgical consciousness, in the rich and explicit teaching of the Fathers of the Church.

Universal priesthood implies no opposition to the functional priesthood of the clergy. The latter is not all an emanation of the laity, a delegation of the congregationalist type. The Church has received a hierarchical structure from the institution of the college of the Twelve in conformity with the divine plan. The People of God is differentiated by God in its "priestly principle", by means of charismatic ministries. The episcopate is chosen from among the people; it is of its priestly flesh and blood; it does not form a structure above, for it is an organic part of the body, of the ontological unity of all its members. Its origin is divine and it is exercised by virtue of apostolic succession. Every candidate is advanced by God: "I have chosen you, and have appointed you." [123] The sacramental power of celebrating the mysteries, and above all, of being an apostolic witness to the eucharist, and the power of promulgating doctrinal definitions—*charisma veritatis certum*—belong to the episcopate in virtue of the apostolicity of the Church. There is also the pastoral charism of leading the body, the royal priesthood, toward the glorious parousia. As a living image of Christ, the bishop has only one true power, that of charity, and

[123] John 15, 16.

only one true force of persuasion, and that is his martyrdom. As these beautiful words declare magnificently: "We are not the masters of your faith, but the servants of your joy."

We can clearly see the essence of the Eastern tradition; it is neither an anti-clerical egalitarianism nor a division by the clergy of the one body into two parts, but the sacerdotal participation of all in the one divine priest by means of two priesthoods. Each one is established by God, and it is this divine origin that lifts them out of this world and out of all profane perspective.

What is gathered in the only one, Christ, the unique priest, is spread throughout the whole body; the priest goes toward the kingdom and the universal priesthood of the priests. The passover and the parousia have not yet occurred; from this comes the co-existence of the two priesthoods, without confusion or separation, and outside any impossible opposition. It is in the differentiation of charisms and ministries that the one Christ is realized.

Thus the tradition does not lead to confusion, but decisively affirms the equality of nature: all are, before everything else, equal members of the People of God. By baptism, "the second birth", all are already priests, and it is in the heart of this priestly equality that the functional differentiation of charisms is produced. It is not a new "consecration", but an ordination for a new ministry of one who was already consecrated, already changed in his nature once for all, having already received his priestly character.

The sacrament of the *anointing by chrism* (confirmation in the West) establishes all the baptized in the same hieratic, priestly order. From this equality, some are chosen, withdrawn and established by a divine act, as bishops and presbyters.[124] A *functional difference* of ministries suppresses all ontological difference of nature and makes all separation between clerics and laymen impossible. Balsamon, a canonist of the 12th century, mentions the opinion that episcopal ordination brings with it a plenary absolution from sins, which would make of it a "second baptism" and

---

[124] The New Testament uses the term πρεσβύτερος to designate the particular ministry (the clergy) and keeps the term ἱερεύς for the priesthood of the laity. This Greek word designated the Jewish priesthood. Christ abolished the *hierus* as a distinct caste. All Christians have become *hiereis*, priests of the royal and universal priesthood.

would thereby change its nature. Such a doctrine has never been accepted by tradition, for it would institute a difference in nature between bishops and the faithful. The possibility of reducing a priest to the lay state with the authorization of conjugal life demonstrates just the contrary. In this case, the cleric sets aside the functional ministry and remains a priest of the universal priesthood; he does not undergo, either before or after, any ontological change. This affirmation stands out more sharply in the presence of two traditions which express, each in its own order, the principle of "divine paternity". One goes back to St. Ignatius of Antioch,[125] for whom every bishop is a "father" by reason of his liturgical function; by water and the Spirit he generates divine sonship.[126] Another tradition goes back to the "fathers of the desert". They were great spiritual laymen, whose charisms were not functional, but personal. A spiritual father, *pneumatikos patēr,* was a "theodidact", taught by God and guided by the Spirit. Though simple monks, they were the spiritual fathers of everyone.

Thus, if the bishop participates in the priesthood of Christ by his sacred function, every lay person does so by his very being; he participates in the unique priesthood of Christ by his *sanctified being,* by his *sacerdotal nature.* In view of this dignity, of being a priest in his very nature, every baptized person is sealed with the gifts, anointed with the Holy Spirit in his very essence. Every lay person is the priest of his existence; he offers in sacrifice the totality of his life and of his existence.

A close correspondence between the "initiation" of the faithful (baptism and anointing) and the ordination of priests confirms this. In fact, the prayer for the eighth day after baptism mentions "the imposition of the hand of God" that establishes the baptized in "the dignity of his sublime and heavenly vocation". The white color of the baptismal tunic is the color of the priesthood in the two covenants. We can understand that for practical reasons only the clergy have kept it. The rite of tonsure signifies the total consecration to ecclesial service; therefore, all, clerics and laity, are set aside for the things of God; all are consecrated. For a child

---

[125] *Magn.* 3, 1.
[126] *The Apostolic Constitutions,* II, 26, 4.

of the male sex, an ancient tradition prescribed a procession around the table of the altar, corresponding to the dignity of a priest of the universal priesthood. According to Hippolytus of Rome,[127] the baptized received the kiss of peace (just like a bishop), as one who is worthy of his new state—*dignus effectus est*. In regard to "the white stone" on which is graven the new name,[128] Hippolytus specifies that this name was pronounced during the eucharist; it symbolized admission to the kingdom, it was the name of a new creature, a member of the royal priesthood. The astonishing liturgical relationship of these rites with the ordination of the clergy accentuates strongly the sacerdotal dignity of every baptized person.

The initiation (the three great sacraments of the faithful) introduces each and every one into the order or sacred hierarchy of the people, differentiated solely by functional ministries.

This perfect equality of nature in all the members of the Church corresponds to the fundamentally homogeneous character of Orthodox spirituality. Likewise there exists no separation into the teaching Church and the Church taught, but it is the total Church that teaches the Church, just as it is in the whole of its teaching that the Gospel is addressed to each and all. Prayer, fasting, the reading of the Scriptures and ascetic discipline are imposed on all for the same reason. That is why the laity very exactly forms the state of *interiorized monasticism*. Its wisdom consists essentially in assuming, while living in the world and perhaps on account of this vocation, the eschatological attitude of the monks, their joyous and impatient expectation of the parousia.

As an example of inward monasticism, common to all, we might mention the ancient tradition that looked upon the period of betrothal as a monastic novitiate in order to prepare for "the conjugal priesthood". Thus the crowns of the betrothed, at the time of the Eastern rite of Coronation (the sacrament of marriage), were kept for seven days, and it was then that the priest gave the blessing to put an end to this time of continence for the spouses. Likewise in the Russia of former days, after the ceremony of marriage in the church, the spouses left directly for a convent.

[127] *Trad. Apost.*
[128] Apoc. 2, 7.

They were initiated for a time into the monastic life in order to be better initiated into their new conjugal vocation, their *conjugal priesthood*.

Nicolas Cabasilas, a great liturgist and layman of the 14th century, entitled his treatise on the sacraments, *The Life of Jesus Christ*. John of Cronstadt, a priest of great sanctity in the beginning of the 19th century, described his eucharistic experiences in *My Life in Christ*. All this shows that the true fatherland of Orthodox souls is the Church of the liturgical mysteries. Nicolas Cabasilas even paraphrased the text of the Acts, saying: "It is by the sacraments that we live, that we move and have our being." [129]

The sacrament of anointing by chrism is the sacrament of universal priesthood. On the man newly born in baptism, the Holy Spirit descends to infuse in him the gift of action. The anointing is the sacrament of strength which arms us as "soldiers and athletes of Christ", in order "to render testimony without fear or weakness", to realize the apostolate of charismatic love. St. Cyril of Jerusalem said to the catechumens: "The Holy Spirit arms you for the combat . . . He watches over you as over his own soldier . . . You will stand firm against any opposing power." [130] Every lay person is before all else a combatant.

The sign of the cross made with chrism on all parts of the body (the Eastern tradition) symbolizes the tongues of fire of pentecost. It is accompanied by the sacred formula: "Seal of the gift of the Holy Spirit." It is therefore in his entire being that every lay person is sealed with the gifts; he is an entirely *charismatic* being.

The prayer placed in the heart of the sacrament specifies the aim of these gifts: "That it may please him to serve thee in every act and every word." This is the consecration of one's whole life to the ministry of the laity, a ministry that is essentially ecclesial.

The totalitarian and absolute character of the consecration stands out clearly in the rite of tonsure, a rite that is identical with that performed for one entering a monastic order. The prayer asks: "Bless thy servant who has come to offer thee as first gifts the

[129] N. Cabasilas, *La Vie en Jésus-Christ*, p. 27.
[130] *P.G.*, 33, 996, 1009.

tonsure of the hair of his head." Its symbolic meaning is unmis-
takable—it is the total offering of his life.

The eschatological accent of the prayer reinforces this meaning:
"May he render thee glory and may he have all the days of his
life the vision of the joys of Jerusalem." Thus all the instants of
time are directed to their eschatological dimension; all acts and
words are in the service of the king. In undergoing the rite of
tonsure, every layman is a monk of *interiorized monasticism,* subject to all the requirements of the Gospel.

To the *epiklesis* of the sacrament, to the request for the Holy
Spirit, the heavenly Father answers by sending him who clothes the
baptized person with Christ, "Christifies" him. In the prayer over
the holy chrism, the bishop asks: "Oh God, mark them (those who
are to be confirmed, anointed, made "Christs") with the seal of the
immaculate chrism; they will bear Christ in their heart in order
to be a *dwelling of the Trinity."* We can remark here how the
Orthodox Church centers all in the Trinity; the trinitarian balance
is stressed here: sealed with the Holy Spirit, become a Christ-
bearer, in order to be the dwelling of the Holy Trinity.

For a religious service, the choice of a text is a commentary in
itself. During the sacrament of anointing, the last verses of St.
Matthew's Gospel are read: "Go therefore and make disciples of
all nations." By this reading the Lord's order is addressed to every
confirmed Christian, to everyone of the laity, and it is in order that
he may accomplish this that the sacrament offers him its grace.
"He must preach to others what he has received in baptism." Besides the accredited missionaries, every confirmed person is "an
apostolic man" in his own way. It is by his whole being, and by his
life, that he is called to give constant testimony.

The idea of a passive people is in flagrant contradiction with
patristic ecclesiology; the universal priesthood of the faithful shares
in the three powers—government, teaching and sanctification.

The first Council of Jerusalem in the time of the apostles [131]
united all the elements of the Church—apostles, elders and
brethren. The words, "the Holy Spirit and we have decided", became the sacred formula of the Ecumenical Councils, and this "we"

[131] Acts, 15.

is the collegial we of the body in its totality. It is the bishops that constitute the Council, but they bear within them the whole body, and their supreme power is exercised only on the level of the mystery of the consensus of all; the bishops act *ex consensu ecclesiae*. As the encyclical of the Eastern patriarchs in 1848 states so well: "With us, innovations cannot be introduced either by the patriarchs or by the Councils; for with us, the safeguarding [132] of religion dwells in the entire body of the Church, that is, in the people themselves who wish to preserve their faith intact." [133] Lay persons are not *judges* (*kriteis*) of the faith; the promulgation of doctrinal definitions is the charism proper to the episcopate. On the other hand, laymen are the *defenders* of the faith. The "shield" is the Church in its entirety, and that is why the ability to distinguish truth from error, "to verify and to testify",[134] is given to all. This defense is even the sacred duty of each lay person. We know that the laity played this role at the time of the Arian crisis in the 4th century, and later in the 15th century, but above all, in the 16th and 18th centuries, in the southwestern part of Russia, when the Orthodox brotherhoods saved the purity of the faith and constituted the real ramparts of truth in the face of a faltering episcopate. The *consensus* of the universal priesthood appeals, in the case of a weak episcopate, to the episcopate enlightened by the Holy Spirit.

In the rites of episcopal ordination, the *axios,* or the *final amen* in other services, is like the sacred signature of the body in its totality on every act of the Church. During the liturgy, every one of the faithful is co-celebrant with the bishop; the people participate actively in the eucharistic anaphora, and in the *epiklesis* where the plural is always employed; the priest says in the name of all: *"We* pray thee," and then he is the apostolic witness of the miracle accomplished. The communion of spirit between the celebrant and the assembly is total, corresponding to the word *liturgy,* which means action in common.

In teaching, and this is a fact peculiar to Orthodoxy, the pro-

---

[132] The act of *protecting* and *defending;* the Greek word used here implies the idea of someone who bears a shield.

[133] *Mansi,* 40, 407, 408.

[134] 1 Thess. 5, 19-21.

fessors of theology are for the most part laymen. The ministry of
the Word is linked with the charism of holy orders, but the bishops
delegate to chosen ones among the laity the power of teaching and
of preaching in virtue of their universal priesthood. In the theocratic
society of Byzantium, the emperor had the power of calling Councils, and imperial preaching had a normal place. We know also
the beautiful homilies of Nicolas Cabasilas, a layman and great
liturgist. We can mention, too, the name of Cyril of Philea, an
ardent hesychast, who was married and the father of a family.
In present-day Greece, laymen are sent by the Synod on apostolic
missions; they teach and preach in the churches; here likewise they
exercise their priestly charism.

In a diocese, the councils and the consistories administer temporal
matters. The bishop is a spiritual father, a pastor and a celebrant.
When it happens, as for example in Greece today, that the State
exercises supremacy in the material organization of the Church,
it is because the State, in principle, represents here the Christian
people.

On the plane of sanctification, the monastic state is entirely in-
dependent of ordination.[135] The spiritual direction of the starets is
not linked to the priesthood. The "pneumatics", the "spiritual men",
whether monks or laymen living in the world, and whom the people
call "the men of God" or "the fools for Christ", enjoy a very great
spiritual authority. The people recognize them as directors of conscience; often it is simple monks who are the spiritual fathers of
bishops and patriarchs. This purely charismatic ministry will never
cease to exist in the Church at the side of the ministry of clerics.

The laity forms an ecclesial atmosphere that is, at the same
time, of the world and of the Church. Laymen do not have access
to the power of giving the means of grace (the sacramental power
of the clergy); but, on the other hand, their sphere is "the life of
grace" and "the state of grace". By the simple presence in the
world of "sanctified beings", of "priests" in their very substance,
of "trinitarian dwellings", the universal priesthood of the laity
holds the power of worship in the world. Outside the church walls,

---

[135] The episcopate according to canon law is incompatible with the monastic degree of *mégaloschème*.

lay people continue the liturgy of the Church. By their active presence, they introduce into society and into human relations the truth of the dogmas they live, thus dislodging the evil and profane elements of the world.

In addition to an active participation in the powers of the Church, the Fathers emphasize the triple dignity of the laity. St. Macarius of Egypt says: "Christianity is not at all something mediocre; it is a great mystery. Meditate on your own nobility . . . By the anointing, all have become *kings, priests* and *prophets* of the heavenly mysteries." [136]

The *royal dignity* is of an ascetic nature; it is the mastery of the spiritual over the material, over the instincts and pulsations of the flesh, the freedom from all determination coming from the world. St. Ecumenius expresses it as "kings, by the ascendancy over our passions".[137] St. Gregory of Nyssa says likewise: "The soul shows its royalty in the free disposition of its desires; this is inherent only in a king; to dominate all is the characteristic of a royal nature."

The royal dignity is thus the "how" of existence, the royal quality of dominating, of being one's master and lord. Its "what", its content, is in the *priestly dignity*. St. Paul exhorts us to offer our bodies as a living sacrifice, a "spiritual service",[138] to make of our being and its existence a worship, a liturgy, a doxology. Origen expresses this admirably: "All those who have received the anointing have become priests . . . If I love my brothers even to give my life for them, and I fight for truth even to death . . . if the world is crucified to me and I to the world, I have offered a sacrifice and I become the priest of my existence." [139] With the same meaning, St. Gregory of Nazianzen synthesizes: "We are priests by the offering of ourselves as a spiritual host." [140]

In order to define the *prophetic dignity,* St. Ecumenius gathers all the dignities together: "kings, by dominion over our passions; priests, to immolate our bodies; *prophets,* in being informed of the

[136] *P.G.*, 34, 624B-C.
[137] *P.G.*, 118, 932.
[138] Rom. 12, 1.
[139] *P.G.*, 12, 512-522.
[140] *P.G.*, 35, 498.

great mysteries".[141] St. Theophylactus adds: "prophet, because he sees what eye has not seen".[142] According to the Bible, a prophet is one who is aware of "the designs of God" in the world, one who grasps the providential course of history under the eyes of God. Eusebius of Caesarea, in his *Evangelical Demonstration*,[143] writes: "We burn the prophetic perfume in every place and we sacrifice to him the fragrant fruit of a practical theology." Here is a magnificent definition of the laity: by his whole being, by his whole existence, to become such a living theology—theophanic— the luminous place of the presence of the parousia of God.

In following the patristic tradition, we can draw in broad outlines a certain "type" of lay person. He is above all a man of prayer, a liturgical being, a man of the *Sanctus* and the *Trisagion,* one who sums up his life in these words of the psalm: "I will sing praise to my God while I live." Abbot Anthony [144] speaks of a man of great sanctity, who practiced his profession of medicine in the world; he gave all that he did not need to the poor and sang the *Trisagion* every day, uniting himself to the choir of the angels. He makes us think of the type of saint called *anargyros,* "disinterested"; he practiced his profession as a form of his priesthood, as a priest. He makes us think also of "the good doctor" of Camus —but such as the author must see him now.

Today, in Communistic countries where the Church is more than ever reduced to a single liturgical life, this destitution becomes a powerful appeal to center oneself on the one thing necessary. Just recently, the Russian episcopate exhorted the laity, in default of a regular liturgical life, to become a temple, to continue the liturgy in their existence, to present to men a liturgical countenance and smile. In the tragic conditions of the utmost tension, the Church teaches above all how to pray, how to share in the combat by a silent testimony, how "to listen to the silence of the Word" in order to render more powerful every compromised word.

[141] *P.G.,* 118, 932C-D.
[142] *P.G.,* 124, 812.
[143] *P.G.,* 22, 92-93.
[144] *P.G.,* 65, 84.

According to an old tradition, St. Michael offers on the altar on high "lambs of fire", the souls of martyrs. Their testimony is not necessarily spectacular. As a priest in the world, the layman practices the discernment of spirits and says "no" to every demoniacal enterprise. The others, those who are "under the altar" cry, "How long, O Lord?" [145] The Church can with all its wealth of human culture make a splendid icon of the kingdom of God, but it can also be despoiled even to martyrdom, and "naked follow Christ naked".

During the liturgy, the bishop collects the prayers and the gifts of the faithful and bears this offering to the Father, and pronounces the *epiklesis* on behalf of all. The presence of the layman in the world is also a perpetuation of the *epiklesis,* which sanctifies every particle of the world, contributes to the peace of which the Gospel speaks, and aspires to the liturgical "kiss of peace". In following the litanies, his prayer is directed to the day ahead, to the earth and its fruits, to the efforts of all men. In the immense cathedral, that is, the universe, man, the priest of his life whether he be workman or scholar, makes of everything a human offering, a hymn, a doxology.

A lay person is an eyewitness of the resurrection of Christ. Such is the teaching of the liturgy and the meaning of the service of Easter night. The liturgical mystery goes beyond the simple commemoration; it "re-presents" the event, even becomes the event. Before the people, the risen Christ appears, and this confers on every one of the faithful the apostolic dignity of a witness.

That is why a layman is also an "apostolic man" [146] in his own way. According to the spiritual writers, he is the one who corresponds to the final words of St. Mark's Gospel: the one who will tread on serpents, cure all sickness, move mountains and raise the dead, if such is the will of God. If he lives his faith simply, he arrives at his final end.

His attitude of recollected silence and humility must also be penetrated with passionate tenderness. St. Isaac and St. John Climacus say that we must love God as a man loves his betrothed,

---

[145] Apoc. 6, 9.
[146] St. Maximus the Confessor, *P.G.,* 90, 913. Cf. Luke 10, 19.

and then to be in love with all of God's creation in order to decipher the meaning of God in everything. According to Merleau-Ponty,[147] "man is condemned to meaning"; we say that he is invited to live his faith, to see what is not seen, to contemplate the wisdom of God in the apparent absurdity of history, and to become light, revelation and prophecy.

Marveling thus at the existence of God, "the world is full of the Trinity", a layman is also slightly mad with the folly of which St. Paul speaks; his is the paradoxical humor of "the fools of Christ", which alone is capable of shattering the portentous gravity of innumerable doctrinaires.

A lay person is also one who is freed by his faith from "the great fear" of the 20th century, fear of the bomb, of cancer, of Communism, of death; whose faith is always a way of loving the world, a way of following his Lord even into hell. This is certainly not a part of a theological system, but perhaps it is only from the depths of hell that a dazzling and joyous hope can be born and assert itself.

Christianity in the grandeur of its confessors and martyrs, in the dignity of every believer, is messianic, revolutionary, explosive. In the domain of Caesar, we are ordered to seek and therefore to find what is not found there—the kingdom of God. This order signifies that we must transform the form of the world, change it into the icon of the kingdom. To change the world means to pass from what the world does not yet possess—for this reason it is still this world—to that in which it is transfigured, thus becoming another thing—the kingdom.

The central appeal of the Gospel is to the Christian violence that alone lays hold of the kingdom. In speaking of St. John the Baptist the Lord indicated violence. Thus St. John is not only a witness of the kingdom; he is already the place where the world is conquered and where the kingdom is present. He is not only a voice that proclaims; he is its voice. He is the friend of the bridegroom, the one who decreases that the other, the divine lover of men, may increase and appear. To be a true lay person is to be one who, by

[147] *Phénoménologie de la Perception*, p. xiv.

his entire life, by what is already present within him, proclaims him who is to come; to be one who, according to St. Gregory of Nyssa, full of "sober intoxication", cries out to every passerby: "Come and drink"; to be one who says with St. John Climacus these words so winged in their joyousness: "Thy love has wounded my soul, and my heart cannot endure thy flames; I go forward, singing to thee. . . ." [148]

The Gospel speaks to us of the violent who bear away the kingdom. One of the sure signs of its approach is the unity of the Christian world. In this expectation of the final accomplishment, hope, the great Christian hope, takes on life. The prayer of all the Churches ascends, formulating an ecumenical *epiklesis,* invoking the Holy Spirit to descend on the possible miracle of unity. This is our ardent desire, our ardent prayer. The destiny of the world rests on the Father's response, but this is dependent on our transparent sincerity and the purity of our hearts.

Jesus Christ, by the total gift of himself, has revealed the perfect priest. As the image of all perfections, he is the supreme bishop; he is also the supreme and unique layman. This is why his priestly prayer bears the desire of all the saints: to glorify the Holy Trinity with one heart and one soul and to unite all men around the one and only chalice.

The divine lover of men awaits us to share this joy, which no longer is only of this world; it already inaugurates the feast of the kingdom.

[148] *P.G.,* 88, 1160B.

6
The Mystic Ascent

St. Paul mentions his ecstasy very briefly and on this occasion gives the essence of the Christian life: "I know a man *in Christ*." [149] The ecstasy is only a special grace, by no means indispensable and never to be sought. On the other hand, every baptized person is "a man in Christ".

We consider that this Pauline expression indicates the mystic state, which means that no one is excluded, and that Christian mysticism is sacramental. [150] No one is a mystic apart from the eucharist. Baptism indeed inaugurates it by the birth of God in the soul. "When the redeemer was born, it was day in the middle of the night." [151] He takes possession of this place and never ceases deepening it. The *Letter to Diognetes* says: "The Logos who is always born in the heart of the saints is born and grows." St. Gregory of Nyssa is more precise: "The child Jesus grows in varous ways according to the measure of each one; he manifests himself as a child, as an adolescent, as a fully grown man." [152] According to St. Maximus the Confessor, a mystic is one in whom the birth of the Lord is best manifested. Likewise St. Ambrose writes: "Each soul that believes, conceives and brings forth the Word of God . . . According to the flesh there is but one mother of Christ, but according to faith, Christ is the fruit of us all." [153] In this way St. Paul defined his pastoral task: "In order that Christ be formed in you." [154]

[149] 2 Cor. 12, 2.
[150] Nicolas called his treatise on the sacraments: *Life in Jesus Christ*.
[151] Kierkegaard, *Papiers*, 1849, p. 122.
[152] *P.G.*, 44, 82, 81.
[153] *In Ev. S. Lucae*, II, 26.
[154] Gal. 4, 19.

In following the progression described by St. Gregory of Nyssa, Christ becomes "a fully grown man" in the human soul when baptism is followed by the eucharist whose influence extends to the whole life of the faithful Christian. "If any man listens to my voice and opens the door to me, I will come in to him and will sup with him, and he with me." [155] It is more than a birth; it is a communion whereby a man "in Christ" becomes a part of his body, his living member. "The same virtue belongs to both tables (one earthly, the other heavenly); the same guest is in both worlds; above, the nuptial palace, here below, a progress toward the nuptial kingdom, and at last to the Spouse. "Great is this mystery," wrote St. Paul to exalt this union; for here is the mystic marriage; the divine Spouse unites himself to his Church [156] and to every human soul.

For the Pauline image of "the head", Cabasilas substitutes "the triumphant and overflowing heart", the inexhaustible source of the treasures of love. That is why the eucharist contains the biblical theme of the mystic espousals. "The man of sorrows" reveals himself as "the man of desires", the eternal magnet and the divine lover of men. Christ alone is the magnet that attracts love and then enters into us in order that we may live again in him. Cabasilas gives clear and simple evidence for this: "The soul thirsts for the infinite. The eye was created for light, the ear for sounds, everything for its end, and the desire of the soul to throw itself toward Christ." [157] The love of God inclines toward earth, and espouses the impulse of the man who ascends.

In his ascent, "the man in Christ" learns the liturgical meaning of history; it suppresses all turning aside and leads him to the hidden reality. The words of St. Paul that God acquired his people "for the praise of his glory" [158] have a parallel in the Apocalypse where the sole occupation of men is "to prostrate and adore". This is because every doxology—eucharist, thanksgiving—"redeems the time", which means that it opens it upon "the eternal present".

[155] Apoc. 3, 20.
[156] N. Cabasilas, *La Vie en Jésus-Christ*, p. 109.
[157] *Ibid.*, p. 79.
[158] Eph. 1, 14.

"Give us this day our daily bread" [159] means that the gifts of salvation and of the kingdom may be granted us even now, even today, here below. It is not a hope for future time, but an immediate requirement, here and now. "We enter paradise *today* when we are poor and crucified," writes Léon Bloy.[160]

St. Matthew's Gospel, in speaking of the last judgment, stresses the decisive character of the present instant. As soon as time merges into eternity, division is done away with, and with it the schizophrenia of syncopated time.

We understand the immense importance of this when we note that the man of history lives outside time. Indeed by a strange alienation, the man of this world lives in the past, in his memories, or in expectation of his future. As for the present moment he tries to escape from it, and exercises his inventive spirit in order "to kill time" better. This man does not live in the here and now, but in reveries of which he is unconscious. An ascetic adage affirms: "The hour that you are living, the task that you are doing, the man whom you are meeting *in this moment,* are the most important in your life." They are so because the past and the future in their abstract dislocation are non-existent and have no access to eternity; the latter converges only toward the present moment and is given only to the one who makes himself totally present at that moment. It is only in these instants that one can attain it and live it under the guise of the eternal present. The liturgical "memorial" clearly teaches this. It suppresses the past that has gone by, makes the totality of history actual, and bears it before the face of the Father, introducing it into the dimension of the present that actualizes the before and after. In the "memory" of the Father, all is present, actual, vibrant with life.

The liturgy, freeing us from the weight of time, a weight caused by its non-existent dimensions, brings the divine presence into a man's soul and permits him to recognize it. It is because Mary Magdalen was looking for her God following an image fixed and stabilized in her, and therefore non-existent, that she did not at once recognize her Lord at the tomb.

[159] More precisely "our bread of tomorrow". See Jeremias, *Parole de Jesus.*
[160] *La Femme pauvre.*

A monk has recently written a book called *Presence of Jesus*.[161] He tells of a day passed with Jesus, a simple day, yet one very different from the ordinary day of a man. One can see in it a kind of osmosis and continuity between the human actions of our Lord and our own acts. Living the Gospel in the humblest things of daily life brings us amazingly close both to Jesus and at the same time to other men. A prayer springs forth spontaneously: "Do not allow thy word to be in my soul as in a sanctuary that is isolated by a grill from the house and the street." [162]

We perceive clearly that it is not at all a question of a "rule of life", often poorly adapted to real life, but of a "style of life", of a spirituality attentive to the mysterious and multiform presence of Christ who awaits us, and who expects from us a certain inventive genius so that we can recognize him and follow him even to hell and beyond. Such a day has the value of a Gospel parable that has been lived; it opens an infinite series, the actual eternity of present moments. If spiritual writers have spoken much of ladders, it is because on these ladders we descend toward men and then, all together, we ascend toward the one who awaits us.

The description of the last judgment is striking in its simplicity, but this does not make it less formidable. The sole accusation is that of being inattentive, insensible to the presence of Christ in every suffering being, in every human person. It is therefore this recognition that Christ expects from man.

"After God, consider each man as God," spiritual men used to say. In place of the usual salutations, they knew how to salute the human face of God in everyone, in every unknown passerby. Abbot Apollos would say to his disciples: "When a pilgrim or a guest comes to visit you, prostrate yourself before him. Not before the man, but before God. For it is said: 'You see your brother, you see your God.' " [163] Such an attitude is never a recipe or a rule, but a *style* that structures man from within and expresses an unquenchable thirst for Christ. One who knows how to say to each one, "my

[161] A monk of the Eastern Church, *Présence du Christ* (Chevetogne, 1960).
[162] *Présence du Christ,* p. 36.
[163] *Apophtegmata Patrum.*

joy", speaks to a man as the dwelling place of God, and that is why his joy is perfect.

The Shepherd of Hermas calls to our attention that whoever omits to help a man in distress will be held responsible for his loss.[164] St. Maximus the Confessor warns us that we shall have to render an account "of the evil we have done, but above all, for the good that we have neglected to do, and because we have not loved our neighbor".[165] If the Gospel condemns every idle word, the agraphon quoted by Didymus of Alexandria goes further: "Of every *good word* that they do not utter, they will render an account on the day of judgment." [166] "At the evening of life, we shall be judged by our love," notes St. John of the Cross.

We know that the piety of the Jews of the Old Testament was formed by hearing. "Listen, O Israel." The Word structures history. But for the same Jews, at the time of the messianic restoration, eschatology replaced hearing by vision. It is no longer, "listen", but "raise your eyes and see". Likewise the Gospel has us hear the words of Jesus, invites us to listen to them, but as soon as history is transcended, "the pure of heart will *see* God". At the moment of his martyrdom, the deacon Stephen *saw* heaven open before his eyes on "the glory of God and of Jesus standing at the right hand of God".

G. Kittel [167] emphasizes that at the moment of the resurrection hearing passed to vision and marked the beginning of the parousia and entrance into eschatological time. A luminous cloud accompanied the Exodus, covered the tabernacle, filled the temple, and revealed the dwelling of the *Shekinah,* the glory of God, and the place of his manifest presence. That is why Moses and Elias, the great visionaries of the Old Testament, accompanied the transfigured Christ, in order to testify to the same divine light. The light of Thabor anticipates that of the parousia and of the world to come.

The spiritual life leads to ineffable contemplation where light is the object, but also the means of vision. The halos of the saints

---

[164] *Simil.* X, 3, 4.
[165] *P.G.*, 90, 936A-B.
[166] Resch, *Agrapha*, 13.
[167] *Die Religionsgeschichte und das Urchristentum.*

in iconography show the luminosity of bodies as being ontologically normative. They are shown on icons, but during life these exterior manifestations are rare, being very special charisms. The spiritual remains interiorized, intense, centered on the heart and on the lifting up of the spirit, visible to God alone.

Seen from above, a saint is already clothed in light, but seen from below, he never ceases to struggle. "We shall not be accused of not working miracles," says St. John Climacus, "but we shall surely have to render an account to God because we have not ceaselessly wept over our sins." [168] St. Isaac declares: "Repentance is the trembling of the soul before the gates of the kingdom." [169]

Not attempting a mediocre imitation, the man following Christ reproduces his image interiorly. "Purity of heart is love for those who fall." [170] The mystic soul dilates and opens wide in a cosmic charity, assumes universal evil, goes through the agony of Gethsemane, and rises to another vision that despoils it of all judgment. "The one who is purified sees the soul of his neighbor." Like sees like. When one sees all men as good and no one as impure, then we can say that he is truly pure of heart. "If you see your brother in the act of sinning, throw about his shoulders the mantle of your love." [171] Such a love is effective because it changes the very substance of things.[172]

It is no longer the passage from passion to continence, from sin to grace, but the passage from fear to love: "The perfect reject fear, disdain rewards, and love with their whole hearts." [173]

The soul is elevated above every determined sign, every representation and every image. The multiple gives place to the one and the simple. The soul, image and mirror of God, becomes the dwelling of God. The mystic elevation orients it toward the kingdom. "If the characteristic of wisdom is knowledge of realities, no one can be called wise if he does not embrace also the things to

[168] *The Heavenly Ladder,* degree 7.
[169] Wensinck, *op. cit.,* p. 310.
[170] St. Isaac, *Sentences.*
[171] St. Isaac, *Sentences, CXV.*
[172] St. John Chrysostom, *P.G.,* 61, 273.
[173] St. Isaac, Wensinck, *op. cit.,* p. 341.

come." [174] "A spiritual man of the latter days," says St. Isaac, "receives the grace that is conformable to him." This is the iconographic vision of "the divine liturgy". The heavenly choir of angels, where the "lost sheep", humanity, has its place, stands before the mystic lamb of the Apocalypse, surrounded by the triple circle of spheres. On the whiteness of the celestial world, the royal purple of the passion stands out, tending toward the splendor of the noon without decline, the iconographic color of divine love clothed in humanity. This is the return of man to his heavenly dignity. At the moment of the ascension of Christ, the angels cried out: "Who is this king of glory?" Now the angels are in profound amazement before this final mystery—the lost sheep becomes one with the shepherd. The Canticle of Canticles sings the espousals of the Word and the dove. Love is the magnet, and the soul, attracted always more violently, casts itself into the luminous darkness of God. One feels the powerlessness of words: luminous darkness, sober ecstasy, well of living water, motionless movement.

"You have become beautiful in approaching my light; your approach has drawn to you a share of my beauty." "Approaching the light, the soul becomes light." [175] At this level, it is not a question of learning about God, but of receiving him and being converted in him. "The knowledge that has become love" is clearly of a eucharistic nature. "The wine that rejoices the heart is called, since the passion, the blood of the vine." "The mystic vine pours out sober intoxication." [176]

"Love is God who throws his arrow, his only begotten Son, after having moistened its threefold point with the vivifying Spirit; the point is faith which not only introduces the arrow but the archer with it." [177]

The soul transformed into a dove mounts always higher—grace upon grace. "Having once put your foot on the ladder on which God had leaned, do not cease to go up . . . each rung leads to one beyond." [178] It is Jacob's ladder.

[174] St. Gregory of Nyssa, *P.G.,* 45, 580C.
[175] St. Gregory of Nyssa, *P.G.,* 44, 869A.
[176] *Ibid.,* 828B-C.
[177] *Ibid.,* 852A-B.
[178] *Ibid.,* 401A-B.

To meet man come "not only the angels, but the Lord of the angels". "But what can I say of what is ineffable; what the eye has not seen, what the ear has not heard, what has not entered into the heart of man to conceive, how can all that be expressed in words?" [179]

Every movement ceases; prayer itself changes in nature. "The soul prays outside prayer." [180] It is hesychy, the silence of the spirit, its repose above all prayer, the peace that surpasses all peace. It is the face-to-face vision extended over eternity, when "God comes into the soul and the soul goes forth to God". In this frontal meeting with the one who has already come, man finally becomes in himself such as divine eternity has changed him. Having arrived at the most desirable end:

"He is separated from all, and united to all;
Impassible, and of a sovereign sensibility;
Deified, and he esteems himself the off-scouring of the world;
Above all, he is happy,
Divinely happy. . . ." [181]

[179] St. Symeon the New Theologian, *Homelie,* XC.
[180] St. Isaac, Wensinck, *op. cit.,* p. 118.
[181] Evagrius, *Le Traité d'oraison.* See J. Hausherr, *Les leçons d'un contemplatif* (Paris, 1960), p. 187.